Murd
&
Mystery
Trails of
Northumbria

by
Clive Kristen

Casdec Ltd

Dedication

To my wife Maureen. Living with me must be murder. It's a mystery why she puts up with it.

Published by Casdec Ltd
22 Harraton Terrace
Birtley
Chester-le-Street
Co. Durham
DH3 2QG

Tel: (091) 410 5556
Fax: (091) 410 0229

Written by Clive Kristen

First Published May 1993

Views and opinions expressed in this book are those of the author and are not to be attributed to the publishers.

ISBN 0 907595 84 7

The Water Mill, Brinkburn

Author's Note

Dear Murder and Mystery Trailer,

This book is a companion volume to the Ghost Trails of Northumbria books. In many ways it could have been Ghost Trails III - the approach is the same but the focus of material is slightly different.

The book contains five further 'tour and explore' trails linked by themes which include murders, mysteries and the supernatural. These trails have been constructed to take best advantage of the great natural beauty of the region, and to bring to life Northumbria's rich historical and cultural heritage

The 'touring times' suggested for each trail are based on a fairly brisk schedule. For those who prefer a more relaxed pace each trail can be conveniently broken down into sections. The Trail Guides provided with each section are intended only to help make sense of the text. They are not to scale and should not be regarded as an adequate substitute for a good map. One major difference in this book from other Trails titles is that two of the five sections are urban routes best tackled on foot.

Whilst every effort has been made to produce accurate historical and topographical detail, the reader will understand that information about the more distant past is often patchy and conflicting versions of stories are common.

In an attempt to make sense of this dilemma the book tries to balance traditional and eye witness accounts with archive and historical material and the common sense of local knowledge. When it has been necessary to select one version of a story from several, contemporary and local accounts have taken precedence.

The historical notes are intended to fill out detail where it has not been appropriate to do so within the main body the text. This final section also corrects a measure of imbalance.

I am indebted to archivists and librarians in Britain and abroad without whose patience and perseverance this would have been a very much slimmer volume. I am also grateful to the many people who have written to me with information and suggestions. Most of all I thank my wife Maureen, for her continued encouragement, compiling and mapmaking skills. Again the historical glossary is mainly her work.

Clive Kristen
March 1993

The Writer

Former teacher and lecturer, CLIVE KRISTEN, joined the ranks of professional writers four years ago.

He spent the first two of those years working as a copywriter and journalist and trying to convince a regional publisher that the time had come to create an updated list similar to the one developed by Frank Graham 30 years ago. Enter Casdec and the far sighted Tom Moffat MBE.

Clive is a regular contributor to a number of national publications but is best known in the region as an outspoken freelance news and feature writer for the NORTHUMBERLAND GAZETTE. In addition to the best selling GHOST TRAILS OF NORTHUMBRIA, another companion volume to this title - MORE GHOST TRAILS OF NORTHUMBRIA - has been inflicted on the world at the same time.

The author has also recently completed 'VENTURES INTO EUROPE', a HOW TO guide, offering independent advice to those considering a permanent escape to France.

A first novel, FROST AND FIRE, is in preparation. Clive's plans for the future include further contributions to the TRAILS series and a book about some of the fascinating NORTHUMBRIAN historical characters that have been rediscovered whilst researching the TRAILS.

The Photographer

DUNCAN ELSON is well established as one of the region's leading portrait and landscape photographers.

His atmospheric photography for GHOST TRAILS OF NORTHUMBRIA has been matched in this latest volume. Duncan has also contributed the pictures to the second CASDEC book in the series - MORE GHOST TRAILS OF NORTHUMBRIA.

He is now working with the writer on a new project COQUETDALE NOW AND THEN, a past and present picture album of Northumbria's most beautiful valley.'

Duncan's ambition is to photograph the world's most beautiful women in exotic locations and to become filthy rich on the proceeds. Failing this he will content himself with continuing to produce some of the most striking and original pictures of the Northumbrian landscape with which he is so much in tune.

Duncan's award winning work has qualified him as a Master Photographer and he is a Licentiate Member of the British Institute of Professional Photographers

𝔗he 𝔍llustrator

The cover and map designs again show two creative facets in the wide repertoire of MARK NUTTALL's skills as an illustrator.

His cover for the first GHOST TRAILS book was considered to be an important reason for the impact of the book. Despite the professional jealousy this caused Mark was nevertheless invited to illustrate the next two volumes in the series.

Mark's relationship with the author began with an unfortunate encounter a Lancashire classroom. The author was the English teacher : the illustrator the pupil. Despite this handicap Mark has managed to become semi-literate. His respect for the author is indicated by the fact that he keeps a picture of him mounted below the cistern of the smallest room in his cottage.

Mark, who is currently working in graphic design for television, is also noted for his distinctive cartoon strips. He is presently illustrating a book of Rubenesque drawings inspired by his life's partner, the voluptuous Helen.

Tynan Weir.
March 1993.

Contents

Taking Care in the Countryside

Most of the sites in this book can be accessed from public rights of way. Where this does not happen visitors can get a good impression of a site from suggested viewpoints

Much of the land is farmed, and should be treated with respect. In a few cases, access is restricted and the necessary consents should be obtained. Special care is required during the lambing season and visitors are requested to follow the guidelines of the country code. Please follow footpaths, close gates, and keep dogs under close control. Litter is unsightly and can cause injury and suffering to animals.

Some of the buildings mentioned are private homes. Please do not trespass or behave intrusively. Property owners have been generous in the information they have provided. Please ensure that their right to quiet and privacy is preserved.

These tours are designed for the motorist and the semi-fit walker. Please remember that Northumbrian weather can be unpredictable - even in summer. It is suggested that visitors do not set out on a countryside walk alone. Adequate footwear and a waterproof garment are necessities. A good map and compass are also highly recommended.

The Author

The Author, Clive Kristen

𝔗hrough 𝔗he 𝔈ye 𝔒f 𝔗he 𝔓hotographer

Murders and mysteries, who needs them? Judging by their popularity, it seems we all do.

Having taken the photographs for two volumes of Ghost Trails, this latest venture was a special challenge. As all the great detectives say, you learn something new about each incident by returning to the scene of the crime. Strangely, this seems to be as true for the 11th. century as the 20th. The lie of the land and the position of the buildings are more than a permanent record of the past. They help to make sense of it. They help to explain what happened.

The photographer, either amateur or professional, gains a great deal from trying to bring the past into focus. One angle may reveal nothing. Another becomes part of the story itself. You become involved with what you see because of tales associated with it. Even the most broken down ruin is somehow more important because of what happened there.

As you follow these trails why not make your own photographic record? Make sure your lens will take in as wide an angle as possible. It is the only way to capture as much as possible of the spectacular Northumbrian landscape. Look for unusual angles and approaches to subjects. I've been known to balance precariously in trees, on walls, and even on litter bins, to get exactly the picture I want. Whilst I don't recommend taking this kind of risk, it proves an important point - planning pictures - rather than taking snaps - is most commonly the difference between success and failure.

Duncan Elson with another award-winning picture

These trails are not to be rushed. If you prepare properly for your days out, I'm sure you'll enjoy them as much as I did.

Duncan Elson
(Master Photographer)
Rothbury. April 1993.

No. 1
The Hermitage
And The
Long Pack

This linear motoring tour takes about five hours

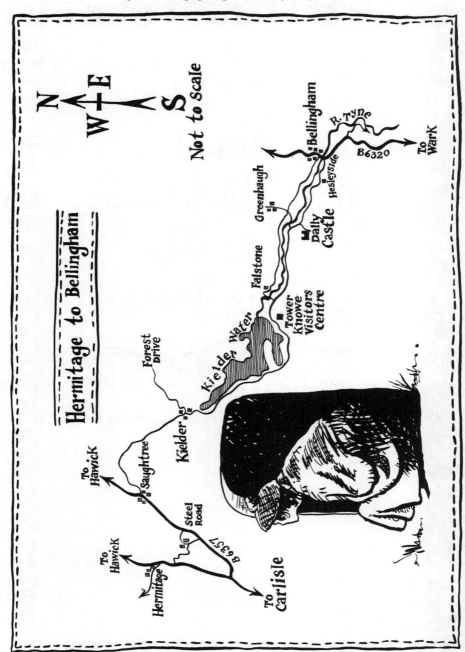

Hermitage to Bellingham

Not to scale

N
W ⊥ E
S

To Wark
R. Tyne
Bellingham
B6320
Greenhaugh
Hesleyside
Falstone
Dally Castle
Tower Knowe Visitors Centre
Kielder Water
Forest Drive
Kielder
Saughtree
To Hawick
Steel Road
B6357
To Hawick
Hermitage
To Carlisle

A Turbulent History

Much of the turbulent history of the borders focuses on the great families who have ruled the land during the last seven centuries. Hermitage Castle, which is in the care of Historic Scotland, amply reflects this. It is a first Trails foray over the border, but one that was just too spectacular to be missed. It is one of the best visual reminders in all the border country of the uncertainties of the medieval world.

The castle is found in a remote corner of Liddlesdale - a minor road off the B6399. Hawick is to the north and Newcastleton to the south. The parking area is by Hermitage Water. Cross the footbridge and enjoy the short walk to the castle.

Hermitage Castle is truly a grim reminder of the past. It was designed as a functional stronghold, rather than a residence. The layout had the advantage of giving attackers as little cover as possible.

It is formed from two rectangular buildings facing each other across a courtyard. The artificial green bank on the approach was once a gun platform.

The Most Evil Of Men

Nicholas de Soulis, a Norman Knight, built a tower here in the 13th. century. Early in the 14th. century his descendant Lord William Soulis plotted against Robert the Bruce. He paid the price by languishing in Dumbarton Castle.

His death provoked strong suspicions. According to a popular ballad Lord William died the most dreadful of deaths - he was boiled in lead. This apparently was the only way to kill him. Lord William it seems was a magician whose powers made him invulnerable to the more conventional tools of murder.

His real fate is unknown. A violent death was certainly richly deserved. As Sheriff of Roxburgh Lord William had earned a reputation for cruelty that ranks him in the Sadists' Premier League. He had a selection of torture instruments in permanent readiness in his dining room so he could enjoy practical demonstrations of their use as he ate.

His name became synonymous with evil. He terrorised the district and arranged the 'disappearance' of many of those who resisted his will.

An Infamous Murder

The most infamous crime was the murder of Cowt of Kielder.

The border chieftain, Cowt or Colt of Kielder earned his name for his massive strength. He was not a large man but it was said that he 'could lift and carry a greater weight than any man in his day'.

Cowt and Lord Soulis were natural rivals. Their castles were placed on opposite sides of a border that contained large tracts of disputed land.

When Cowt received a dinner invitation from Lord Soulis he was naturally suspicious. His wife begged him not to go. A noted seer - the Brown Man of the Moors* - also warned him what his fate would be if he put himself in Lord Soulis's hands.

Finally though, Cowt accepted. He believed in the strength of his own arm and the conventions of border hospitality.

" Could any man," he declared, " be so foul as to invite his neighbour to dine and still seek to take his life? "

The answer of course was yes. But the Lord of Kielder at least took sensible precautions. A dozen of his finest men travelled with him. He wore a 'charmed' suit of armour that could not be pierced by sword or arrow, and a necklace of rowan berries - a sure antidote to spells and evil spirits.

Some say that the Brown Man told Lord Soulis of Cowt's 'insurances'. In the end it made little difference. When Lord Soulis drew his sword, Cowt's men were unable to defend their master. A spell, a poison, or perhaps the medieval equivalent of superglue held them in their places at the great table.

But whatever trickery Lord Soulis had devised was not enough to make the Tyneside Hercules an easy victim.

In swashbuckling Hollywood style he fought his way out of the castle and managed to reach his horse. He escaped as far as the bridge which crossed the burn, but then his horse slipped and Cowt was thrown into the river. Weighed down by his armour and the scrum of Soulis's men who leapt on top of him, his fate was now certain. His strength was sapped and the 'magic' armour proved no protection against death by drowning.

The place where this happened is still known as Cowt of Kielder's Pool. It is close to the ruins of the 13th. century chapel - very likely the site of the earlier hermitage. A large mound nearby is said to mark the Lord of Kielder's grave.

A Famous Owner

Hermitage Castle was once owned by James Hepburn, the fourth Earl of Bothwell.

Bothwell was described by Cecil's correspondents as 'the naughtiest man that liveth and much given to detestable vices'. But Bothwell was more than simply evil, he was one of the great schemers of his age.

An Extraordinary Career

On route to a mission in France in 1560 he seduced and possibly married Anne Thorssen in Denmark. Soon he deserted her.

Seven years later they met again. Anne was naturally enough seeking revenge. Somehow Bothwell managed to placate her with the gift of a ship and a promise of money.

This would be extraordinary enough. But what had happened during those missing seven years is almost the stuff of fantasy.

Bothwell was ordered out of Edinburgh in 1561 because he had become the source of civil unrest that lead to orchestrated riots. In the following year he plotted against Queen Mary and was brought back to the capital to be imprisoned in the castle. He came close to the shadow of the axe but made his peace with the queen and promised to be useful.

In 1564 he was shipwrecked on Holy Island, captured at Berwick, and imprisoned in the Tower of London. After a brief exile in France he successfully evaded Queen Elizabeth's ships and returned to Scotland to help Queen Mary put down the Murray rebellion of 1565.

In February 1566, although already 'handfasted' to Janet Betoun, he married the Earl of Huntley's daughter, Jane. Within months of this joyous event he secured his position as Queen Mary's closest advisor and lover.

In October 'Little' Jock Elliot, one of the most notorious of the border reivers, did his best to end Bothwell's career with a knife. As he lay 'between life and death' at Hermitage Castle Queen Mary rode fifty miles from Jedburgh in the foulest of weather to be with him. He made a rapid recovery. She was gravely ill for several weeks.

On Sunday 9th February 1567 he organised the Kirk o' Field explosion that ended the life of the Queen's estranged husband, Lord Darnley. This still ranks alongside the work of Burke and Hare* and the Massacre of the Macdonalds at Glencoe as the most callous and dreadful of Scottish murders. When the 'news' was brought to Bothwell at Holyrood he feigned suitable shock and surprise. 'It was a catastrophe,' he said,'that had doubtless been caused by lightning'.

On 24th. April he abducted a not unwilling queen and carried her off to his castle at Dunbar. He was granted the necessary divorce and a papal dispensation for the new marriage. The legally questionable ceremony took place on May

15th. Three days previously Bothwell had been created Duke of Orkney and Shetland.

But this was the beginning of the end. Lords Protestant and Catholic united at last to secure his downfall. A large army was raised against him.

He retreated to Dunbar where Mary joined him. They quickly recruited their own troops but their army deserted in droves at Carberry Hill on 15th. June. They surrendered and returned to Dunbar where Bothwell said a sorrowful goodbye to the queen.

After a short stay in Orkney and Shetland Bothwell returned to Norway. This is where he again encountered Anne Thorssen. Typically he escaped her revenge and settled in Denmark.

But the downfall of Mary, Queen of Scots was also his own. In 1573 he was imprisoned at Dragsholm. He died insane in April 1578.

Witch Bothwell?

The next owner of Hermitage Castle, Francis Hepburn, was the Earl's successor.

This new Bothwell used the castle for raids into English territory. In 1589 he lost royal favour and was imprisoned for his part in an uprising. In the same year he was imprisoned on a charge of witchcraft.

He escaped and became an outlaw. Two years after an abortive attempt to seize Holyrood Palace he finally captured King James and forced him to promise a pardon and the restoration of lands.

Surprisingly perhaps the king kept his promise. Bothwell however relapsed into his lawless ways. Finally he was forced to take refuge in France, then Italy. He died in Naples in 1614.

Left To Rot

The basement of the north-east tower contains a small room - just five feet by six - which could only be entered from above. This is the castle's famous oubliette.

It is the site of a murder most foul. Sir William Douglas threw his enemy, Sir Alexander Ramsay, into this hole.

Unlike the Bothwells, Douglas had a reputation as 'a flower of chivalry'. However Ramsay had become Sheriff of Teviotdale, and this was a post that Douglas greatly coveted.

Douglas attacked the sheriff as he left the court at Hawick. Poor Ramsay was wounded by his enemy before he could defend himself.

What happened next changed Douglas's reputation from white knight to black heart. The wounded man was thrown into the oubliette and left to starve. Douglas would listen to no protests. It is said that Ramsay survived for 17 days by feeding on grain that trickled down from the store above.

Years later when the oubliette was opened. They found a bridle, a saddle, a sword, and a pile of oat husks next to the grey bones.

Across The Border

From Hermitage Castle turn south to Newlands. A second left turn by a green shack leads to a minor road. There are fine views over Hartsgarth Fell to the west.

The road skirts Arnton Fell to Steele Road, a hamlet of former railway cottages.

Poetic Justice

Whilst the railway was being constructed this was a small but thriving community where the workers were known to enjoy a pint or two of beer after a hard day's work. Unhappily this sometimes led to arguments. One brawl had fatal consequences.

Will McCaffrey and Tam MacCloud were both rivals for the affections of a local farmer's daughter. One drunken night it was decided the right to court her would be decided on a hand of cards. MacCloud won but McCaffrey refused to accept the decision. They played a second hand and MacCloud won again. McCaffrey accused MacCloud of cheating. A fight began.

It is not clear what happened next. Some say McCaffrey stabbed his rival in the belly, others that MacCloud inflicted the injury on himself in their drunken struggle. Tam MacCloud staggered into the street and collapsed. He was carried to his bed but it was already too late to call a doctor. The local barber managed to quench the flow of blood but Tam MacCloud was dead in less than half an hour.

The community closed ranks and the incident was reported as an accident. Will McCaffrey disappeared before Tam MacCloud was cold.

The farmer's daughter became distracted when she heard the news. Some weeks later she too was found dead in a snow filled gully on a nearby hillside. She had died of exposure.

That would have been the end of the matter but for a strange ghostly intervention.

Some folks in Steele Row who sought revenge made enquiries as to McCaffrey's whereabouts. He seemed to have vanished for ever.

But a year later, almost to the day, a visitor climbing the road towards the cottages was alarmed to hear a strange female voice ringing in his ear.

" McCaffrey's away to Liverpool", the voice said.

The visitor spun around but could see no one. As he reached the cottages he heard the voice again.

" Tell them McCaffrey's away to Liverpool", it said.

Again he could see nothing.

The visitor was confused and concerned. He told his host what had occurred. His host took it seriously enough to tell the minister. The minister warned of unwelcome investigations that would follow if the whole story was now passed on to the authorities. Furthermore, he reasoned, they would hardly be galvanised into action after a tip off from a phantom voice.

The minister talked at length with the visitor who had heard the voice. He was impressed by the way the man told his story. The minister wrote a discreet letter to a colleague in Liverpool.

The reply convinced him not only that the voice had spoken the truth, but that poetic justice had caught up with Will McCaffrey.

The letter referred to a body recently pulled out of a river. But the real cause of death of Will McCaffrey's was not drowning, but a deep jagged stab wound in his stomach.

It seems that the wound was inflicted in a skirmish outside a hostelry on Waterloo Road in Liverpool. The body had later been transported to the nearby Trafalgar Dock and dumped in the water.

The attackers were never brought to justice.

A Bleak Landscape

Turn left onto the B6357 and follow Liddell Water to Saughtree. Turn right to take the minor road to Kielder.

This is a bleak landscape with much evidence of lime kilns and turf cutting. As you cross the border you enter the massive Border Forest Park.

When you reach the village turn up to a car park above the castle.

Kielder Castle

The castle began life as a shooting lodge for the Duke of Northumberland in 1775. The castle is now in the care of Forest Enterprises. It is worth a visit.

Well thought out exhibitions do much to help the visitor understand the area.

One display area is dedicated to the Kielder Viaduct - ' the finest railway arch in Britain' - constructed in 1867. The viaduct is located at the northern end of the lake.

Another part of the exhibition reflects the history of the castle. The reivers enjoy their own section.

The carefully balanced, sometimes symbiotic relationship between wildlife and forestry is fully explained. A dozen wildlife rangers are employed in the Forest Park, the scale of which is perhaps most vividly measured in roe deer. There are 6000 of them.

There are several excellent forest walks from the castle. One of the best follows the Kielder Burn briefly before becoming a circular forest trail. A pleasing aspect of this walk is the mass of Old Man's Beard on view. This lichen only thrives in unpolluted air.

The Brown Man Of The Moors

The Brown Man of the moors, who advised Cowt of Kielder, is an elusive character. He crops up in a number of local legends, sometimes as seer and sometimes as villain.

He is confusingly similar to the legendary Deugar of Simonside - an evil man-eating dwarf when roused by temper or hunger.*

Brown Man or Deugar clones also turn up in stories around Elsdon and the Harwood Forest.** This is around 15 crow fly miles from Kielder so it is not unlikely that the stories have a common root.

Half a mile to the south-east of the castle is a long bronze age barrow and cairn. The local - probably medieval - name for this is the Devil's Lapful.

It was here that the Brown Man held his 'court'.

Harping Back

Some time after Cowt's death, his famously attractive young widow visited the seer. She wanted to know if she should marry again.

" Marry a man born with 12 fingers, " said the Brown Man mysteriously. The lady, who is sometimes called Rebecca, was distressed by advice that seemed to unreasonably restrict her marriage options. Happily however, such a man put in a fairly prompt appearance.

It was Yuletide and the time of music. The tradition was that the finest young musician in the area was invited to play at the castle.

By local acclaim this was a young man called Robert, who though digitally challenged had put the deformity to good use by becoming an exceptionally fine harpist.

But Rebecca was concerned about marrying beneath her.

" Don't worry about that, " said the Brown Man, " for he has great riches in his hands."

Not long after the nuptial knot was secure Rebecca learnt the truth of this.

Robert played the harp to such effect that even the fairies came for lessons. This became important when the evil Lord Soulis decided it was time for his dinner invitation to be returned.

He arrived at Kielder in determined mood. If his magic had been enough to kill the Cowt, there was little doubt it would also be strong enough to win the favours of his lovely widow. The fact that Rebecca had married again was a trivial matter to Lord Soulis.

But Robert and his fairy friends had other ideas. After the banquet Robert was instructed to play. The fairies, who formed his backing group, helped the young man create such magical notes that the lord and his men were utterly overcome with emotion. Floods of tears flowed from eye to cheek and down to beard. All thoughts of ravishing or reivering floated from their minds.

Lord Soulis left Kielder with only one request - permission to send his finest musician for a crash course of harp lessons. For this kind service he was happy to pay handsomely in gold...

Kielder Water

Kielder Water - the largest artificial lake in the UK - was once a controversial project. Few who see it today believe it has done anything other than add to the natural beauty of Upper Tynedale.

The full story is ably told at the Tower Knowe Visitor Centre.

A Fateful Assignation

Just before the road crosses the Tyne turn right towards Birks and Hesleyside. After half a mile turn right again. A no through road brings you to the ruins of Dally Castle. Access is via a stile just beyond the farmhouse.

The ruins are worth a visit. There is much more than meets the eye from the road below. Essentially what remains is part of the keep and the great wall. There is also a splendid view over the Chirdon Burn below.

Ruined Dally Castle

The castle dates from the early 13th. century when the land was part of the Scottish kingdom. It was given to a knight called David de Lindsay by the sister of King Alexander III.

The castle bred a famous legend.

The sister of a later owner fell in love with her brother's enemy, Gilbert of Tarset. The Lord of Dally was tipped off about their secret meetings and banned his sister from seeing Gilbert again.

But the meetings continued. The Lord of Dally had his sister followed. When he learnt what was happening he lay in wait for Gilbert and pursued him across the heights of Hareshaw Common.

When Lord Dally caught his man a fight of epic proportions began. They were both tall strong men and many vicious blows were exchanged.

Finally Gilbert of Tarset was killed. His enemy's sword point had glanced upwards from his parry and struck him in the throat. Lord Dally made sure of the job by cutting off Gilbert's head.

The place where Gilbert fell was later marked by a cross. The area is still known as Gib's Cross.

Bonny Bellingham

With a population of not much more than 1000 Bellingham is nevertheless regarded as a Northumbrian Town. It is the capital of North Tynedale and the only place of any size for miles around.

Bellingham is noted as a gateway to both the Border Forest Park and the Northumberland National Park. Consequently it is popular with visitors particularly during the summer months. But Bellingham is more than just a

tourist centre, it's a busy small town with a lively market. The regular lamb sales and the agricultural show attract farmers and buyers throughout the region and beyond. Some years ago it was also a noted centre for coalmining and ironworking.

Boer War Memorial, Bellingham

Bellingham has character. It is attractive rather than beautiful in the picture postcard sense, but it is typically Northumbrian. It's the sort of place you go back to again and again.

The small market place features an unusual Boer Wall Memorial. Outside the Town hall there is a mounted Gingall - a kind of musket. This

Another Relic of War

trophy forges an unexpected connection between a local man and the Chinese Boxer Uprising.

A Phantom Fight

A fight of a different kind has been said to take place in the market square.

During the 18th. century there were reports of a skirmish between the King's Men and their deadly rivals, the Ironsides. What is unusual about this conflict is that it took place a century after the English Civil Wars.

It was perhaps a phantom re-enactment of a real event. But the participants in the replay seemed real enough to witnesses until after the last blow was struck. Then both victors and vanquished floated away into the ether.

This phantom fight was seen on several occasions. It was taken seriously enough to encourage local churchmen to join forces and perform an exorcism. This was as unusual, to say the least. It was also successful. There have been no phantom battles reported since 1746.

St. Cuthbert's Church

The church marks one of the temporary resting places of the saint's body on its long journeys around Northumbria.* The earliest evidence of construction is 13th. century but it is has a place in history going back at least two centuries before that.

The building was fired many times during border raids. This may begin to explain the heavily buttressed stone roof. In many ways this rare 17th. century addition can be seen as a case of locking the stable door after the horse has bolted. Nevertheless it has stood the test of time.

Behind the church there is the footpath to St. Cuthbert's - locally Cuddy's - Well. The water taken from here is supposed to have special healing powers. It is still used for Christenings.

Cuddy's Well

A Famous Story

There is a vivid reminder of one of the region's best known stories in the churchyard. It is a gravestone shaped like the pack that was carried by pedlars in the early 18th. century.

The Lang Pack

The Long Pack

The Long Pack incident took place at Lee Hall.

Take the B6320 towards Wark. After two miles a left hand turn takes you on a looping narrow road down towards the Tyne. Keep right at the cattle grid and the road leads you to Lee hall - a large T-shaped bastle styled farmhouse. A millstone is featured as part of the outer wall.

The best known version of the story has a pedlar calling at the hall on a summer's day in 1723.

The family were out, but a maid allowed him to leave his pack and call back later. Two of the other servants noticed movement inside the pack and became suspicious. One of them went for a gun and blasted a round of pellets into the pack.

Lee Hall

The widening circle of blood told its own story. The pack was ripped open. Inside was a young man who was already close to death.

This was a trick that had been played before. If the young man had not been discovered he would have waited until dark before opening the door to his accomplices.

A 'Welcoming Committee' was arranged and the thieves were greeted by a shot gun salute. It is not known how many were injured or killed.

The young man was buried in the churchyard at Bellingham. It is believed that the body was later removed.

* See Ghost Trails of Northumbria

** See More Ghost Trails of Northumbria

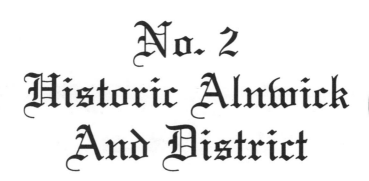

No. 2
Historic Alnwick
And District

This linear tour takes about four hours

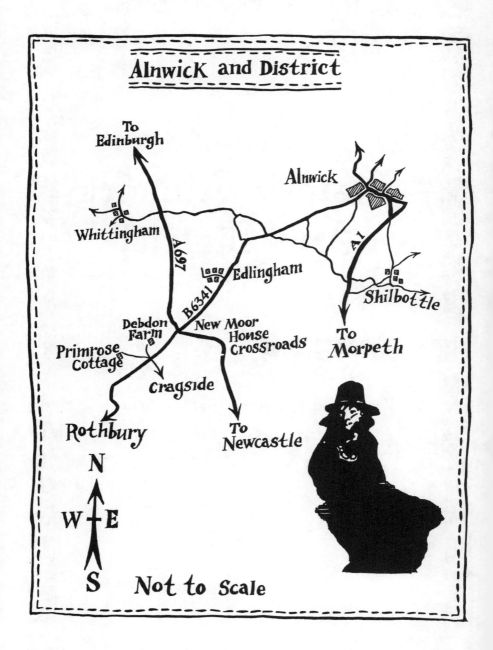

Alnwick and District

To Edinburgh

Alnwick

Whittingham

A697

A1

Edlingham

B6341

Shilbottle

Debdon Farm

New Moor House Crossroads

To Morpeth

Primrose Cottage

Cragside

Rothbury

To Newcastle

N
W—E
S

Not to Scale

$\mathfrak{T}$his tour combines a visit to Alnwick and a brief motoring tour of towards Rothbury.

The Best Touring Centre

Alnwick is perhaps the best centre for touring rural Northumberland. It is situated just four miles from the sea and midway between Berwick and Newcastle. Wooler, the gateway to the Cheviots, is just 18 miles away.

Historic Alnwick

The town has long been an important strategically. It is a fortified town that retains much of its medieval character. The annual week long fair is perhaps the best time to capture the atmosphere of the past. It is not just the town that is dressed up for the occasion, but many of its people wear elaborate costumes.

The first motte-and-bailey castle was built in Alnwick soon after the Norman Conquest.

In 1093 King Malcolm of Scotland was killed near the town. A later Scottish king, William the Lion, was taken prisoner after attacking the castle.

In 1433 the people petitioned King Henry VI for permission to construct town walls. This project took more than 50 years.

Alnwick became the County Town of Northumberland during the reign of Edward VI. During the English Civil Wars the town remained strictly neutral but at the time of the Jacobite rebellions sympathy was very much with the exiled Stewarts.

In more recent times Alnwick became an important stopping point on the Edinburgh to London stagecoach route. The advent of rail helped to consolidate the town's position as a communications centre.

The Tenants' Response

The town visit begins at the Tenantry Column on Bondgate Without.

The official history of the column is that it was built in 1816 as a mark of appreciation to the Duke who had lowered rents during difficult economic times. The money was provided by '1000 grateful tenants'.

It is generally accepted that the truth is rather different. Rents had been doubled and redoubled during previous years and the modest reduction was regarded as derisory. The Duke even had to make a contribution to ensure that the project was completed.

The Tenantry Column

The column has therefore earned the name 'The Farmers' Folly'. It is a symbol of subversion and anti-establishment thinking. It is also a permanent reminder of the sometimes uneasy relationship between the county's great landowners and their tenants.

The Hotspur Tower

The Hotspur Tower stands at the entrance to the Bondgate. It was built in 1480. It is the only one of the original gates that survives.

The tower divides Bondgate Within (the walls) from Without. 'Bond' derives from 'bondagers' - often loosely interpreted as the farmworkers who walked through this gate each day on their way to the fields.

More accurately, a bondager in Northumberland was a female outworker married to a farm labourer. After the plague in particular there was a shortage of field workers. Men living in tied cottages were forced as a condition of tenancy to supply several weeks unpaid labour to the landowner. It was normally the women in the family who undertook this work. Indeed it was a kind of bondage, or slave labour.

In this sense the Bondgate is a reminder of the realities of the late medieval world. The Tenantry Column represents the modest progress made in tenants' conditions by the 19th. century. There are those who would argue that even at the end of the 20th. century very little had changed.

Life And Death At The Poor House

A short detour up the hill from the tower brings you to the Green Batt. The name dates from the time when men were compelled by law to become skilled archers. 'Batt' is a dialect version of 'butt' - the place where archery was practised.

The Poor House was on the north side of Green Batt. It contained six dormitories, a hospital and a special dead house for corpses.

The work rooms were in the attic. The work was stupefyingly dreadful - mainly the teasing of oakum and spinning.

In the old house adjoining there were 'convenient rooms for the Keeper', a dining room, two cells for lunatics, and several small apartments.

In 1810 there were 22 'poor persons' in the main house, as well as 33 children under the age of five. 323 more local people were receiving 'out of house' relief. The poor house mortality rate was one death per 11 persons per annum. The local average was one in 47.

Living in these conditions perhaps explains why murder was a not uncommon crime during the first half of the 19th. century. The poorhouse keepers themselves were greatly despised. The official account of an murderous attack on one former keeper - carried out by two inmates armed with kitchen knives - states that this was the work of lunatics. A second contemporary account hints more at revenge for ill treatment. The exact circumstances of the attack are unknown.

An Innocent Activity

Bondgate Within leads towards the town centre and market place.

The first of Alnwick's market charters was granted in the 12th. century. Northumberland Hall has a street level area known as the shambles. This is a 19th. century building on the site of butchers' market stalls.

The Town Hall dates from the 18th. century. The old clock was particularly important. It was an offence to begin trading before 11 am on a Saturday.

The Market Cross, Alnwick

The present market cross stands on a much older base. For centuries the town crier - the official news service of the day - made his announcements from these steps.

Bull Baiting, described by one local worthy as 'an innocent and pleasurable pastime' was banned in 1835. The practise was to test the bravery of dogs by setting them on a bull. Much money changed hands on the outcome. The dogs were specially bred for the 'sport' with great power in the forward part of their bodies and jaws. The bulldog and larger bull mastiff can be traced back to these times.

Things did not always go according to plan. This account from 1783 makes sobering reading :

' The bull was that enraged he threw down two tradesmen, one of whom had his leg broken and the other received a severe wound in the head. Another bull broke loose and galloped wildly through the streets tossing dogs lifeless in the air and trampling those who blocked his way. The market was crowded with men

The Pottergate Tower, Alnwick

and women. They were clustered in the windows, on the cross, the town hall stairs, and in the shambles.'

Cock fighting was 'practised' between Christmas and Easter. There were at least a dozen cock pits around Alnwick. The biggest was near to the Pottergate Tower. Sometimes the cock fight was combined with other pleasures. The most notorious 19th. century hostelry - the Angel - also featured skittles and 'games of chance'.

A Cure For The Common Scold

The ducking stool - revived for the modern festival - was used for 'common scolds'. Margaret Pearson and Jane Scott were subjected to this indignity in 1650. Both were notorious for their high decibel voices. Margaret Pearson was also said to be a witch. Records do not reveal if this attempt at behaviour modification was successful.

The ducking stool once had a more sinister use. By 1611 witch prosecutions around the country had reached epidemic proportions. It was perhaps inevitable that there would be victims in Alnwick.

One victim of the hysteria was a Shilbottle woman called Annie. Rumours had been circulating for some time that she was a witch and magistrates reluctantly gave permission for her to be tried at the ducking stool.

The theory was that water would reject those who had truck with the devil. A large crowd gathered to witness the 'trial'. The old woman was unable to hold her breath for long enough on the third immersion. Clumsy attempts were made to revive her but her lungs had filled with the foul water. She was pronounced 'not guilty' but died without regaining consciousness.

Revenge Or Not?

An interesting recent theory is that this trial by water was orchestrated for revenge.

It is said that Annie's daughter, Esther, had been raped by a local farmer's son two years earlier. Bruising to her face, neck and breasts, together with the tearing of her clothes, left little doubt that a crime had been committed.

But no action was taken. Esther's attacker suggested typically that she was a woman of easy virtue who had become outraged that he had not paid enough. The bruises, he argued, were an occupational hazard for which he was not responsible.

The authorities accepted this. In the 17th. century rape was not considered to be a crime of any significance, unless committed against a woman of high social standing.

But the townswomen were furious and five of them took matters into their own hands.

They found the young man working in a field near High Buston. They faced him again with his crime. His response was to make lewd suggestions to two of the women.

They became angry, grabbed him and pulled him to the ground. Next they secured his wrists and began to build a fire.

He continued to taunt them. He threatened revenge for their misuse of him. He reminded them of his family connection to the local judiciary.

But the irons were already heating in the fire. When they were ready to the ground by three of the women, a fourth opened his clothing, and the fifth placed the hot irons on his chest and genitals.

It was rumoured that the woman who applied the hot iron was Annie - the mother of the rape victim.

The man survived. His criminal inclinations towards women however had undoubtedly been ironed out forever.

The Whisper Of Death

It has been suggested that the rumours of witchcraft against Annie were started as the result of this attack.

But there are problems with this. There is no real evidence that Annie led the attackers, or even that she was with them. Annie was a common name at the beginning of the 17th. century. We cannot be sure that Annie the witch was also Annie the mother of Esther. Finally, the woman who died at the ducking stool was said to be a woman of fairly advanced years. The rape victim, her supposed daughter, was little more than a girl. Whilst it is not impossible, the age gap suggests the connection is unlikely.

A View From The Street

Any rose tinted view of life in the town should be weighed against this early 18th. century description :

' Pigs ran unringed through the streets, dunghills were on the public highways, and compost was heaped up in the fore street. Butchers killed their sheep at the Shambles in the market place, which was offensive with blood and offal. Dead horses sometimes lay in the street. The current of water was stopped with garbage.'

Sometimes it was not only dead horses that lay in the street. A 16th. century account paints a grim picture :

' The first was an older man, the second younger. They lay at the roadside. Pools of blood ran down the stones and mingled together. Nobody would say what this had been, or what was the cause of it. I encountered resistance to all questions and deemed it prudent to enquire no more. When I returned from my business they lay there yet. The bodies were covered in flies. Birds pecked at the flesh of their faces.'

The Darkest Hour

Although the people of Alnwick were well used to living with uncertainty, the darkest days were probably those of the plague of 1637.

The disease spread from nearby Denwick. Victim's bodies were buried in a large plague pit in a field. The village was virtually depopulated.

In Alnwick the dead were 'conveyed by carts'. The ringing of the bell and the call to 'bring out your dead' continued for almost a year.

The market was moved a mile out of town. The townsfolk lined up on one side of the road and the country folk on the other. They bartered and bargained by shouting across the space between them.

Nutcrack Night

But life was not always miserable, there were many pageants and celebrations too. Few excuses were needed for music and dancing. A regular Shrove Tuesday football match brought ' the able bodied and foolhardy' many miles to join in. Kickoff was always from the gates of the castle.

At one time there were 30 public houses in Alnwick. Many of them were small but each had its loyal customers. Rivalry between these establishments was generally friendly. There were constant games and challenges and each hostelry loudly supported its own champion at the wrestling. Games like bowls and quoits often had their origin in this rivalry. Archery competitions were gradually replaced with something more akin to the modern darts. Halloween featured an unusual medieval pastime that continued well into the 19th. century.

Names were given to nuts before they were placed on the fire. The question was ' did they burn together or fly asunder'. It was intended as a way to test partner compatibility. Today they use computers. Judging by the failure rate of dating agencies perhaps there's something to be said for Alnwick's more traditional method?

Also Of Interest

Before leaving the town centre there are a number of other features of interest.

The cobble stones on Market Street were taken from the beds of the Aln and Coquet. They have proved themselves to be a hard wearing road surface but have turned many an ankle. Cobbles and stilettos are no more historically compatible than the abacus and the computer.

Also on Market Street is St. Michael's Pant. It was built in 1765 to provide the town with a safe source of drinking water. The carving features St. Michael scoring a points victory over a dragon.

The Windsor Of The North

Narrowgate leads towards the castle passing the Old Cross Inn, known as the Dirty Bottles for reasons that are obvious from the window display.*

The castle itself is well worth a visit. It is the northern home of the Duke of Northumberland and has been quite properly described as the Windsor of the

North. Much of Alnwick's turbulent history can be linked to those who have occupied the castle.*

The Horrible Hermit

A recently published version of this story was headlined as 'The Alnwick Zombie'. That seems some way from the truth, but it is nevertheless an enduring myth.

At the time of the bubonic plague an old man - sometimes referred to as a hermit - lived in squalid conditions close to the castle.

The man would certainly have come last in any beauty or popularity contest. He was a dirty, hollow eyed, spindly little man with long range halitosis.

If this was insufficient reason for locals to give him a wide berth, his behaviour made sure of it. He killed and butchered animals in the street. Whilst this was unexceptional at the time it should be added that his favoured diet included those neighbourhood cats and dogs careless enough to wander within his grasp.

When children disappeared the finger of suspicion was pointed in his direction. When a young girl was raped it was said he was responsible. The girl herself was unable to comment on the matter. Her tongue had been cut out. But there was never any hard evidence against him. Certainly he was never brought to account for his 'crimes'. When he died there was great rejoicing.

Farm workers were sent to remove the body. A clinging nauseous smell greeted them as they entered the primitive bothy. But there were greater horrors to follow. The body of the man was wedged in a chair and his hollow eyes were fixed in a dead man's stare. Rigor mortis made him awkward to move. Bones were broken to force him into a coffin. He was buried, despite protests, in the local churchyard.

In the darkness before dawn, several days later, the sexton tripped over an empty coffin. This horror so affected him that he ran from the churchyard and refused to return until accompanied by soldiers with torches. First they found the empty coffin, then the empty grave. But the 'hermit' seemed to have vanished altogether.

In pale early morning sunshine they widened their search. The body was found propped against a tree some distance away.

What we may now see as a deranged trick was the spark that fired local hysteria. It was widely rumoured that the dead man had climbed from the grave unaided. Indeed, in order to prevent this happening again the 'hermit' was re-interred with a small mountain of stones placed on the coffin.

All ills were blamed on the dead man. The plague entered the town walls. A blacksmith was found on open moorland with his throat slit. A child disappeared. Even dogs howling in the darkness were said to be suffering from his special curse.

Finally the church was petitioned to have the body removed beyond the bounds of the parish. A large crowd gathered as spades were once again plunged into the churchyard soil.

If exaggeration is the natural sequel to hysteria, then the imagination of the people of Alnwick knew no bounds. There had been stories of the dead man stalking the streets in his shroud. At other times he changed his form to a familiar - a black cat - and leapt from roofs to sink his teeth into the necks of victims. So it continued, until at the graveside mass hysteria, and possibly some drunkenness, gave way to a final flurry of fantasy.

Some said the dead man had forced his way from the coffin a second time and was climbing up through the stones. A rational explanation - that the great weight pressing on the flimsy coffin lid had splinted and crushed it went almost unheeded. The body had the appearance of having swollen in the ground. Whilst this was not impossible with gallons of water constantly filtering down through the stones, the popular explanation was more Hammer House of Horror. The undead was gorging on the blood of his victims. The corpse was struck by a spade and the bloated form reduced before their eyes. The foul stench was the ' Devil's Breeze'. We would call it methane.

The body was burnt and the ashes thrown into the river.

Henry The Wizard

It was not just the poor who were said to be in league with Satan. In the early years of the 17th. century the ninth earl earned the nickname Henry the Wizard.

Henry was an alchemist who had one of the larger castle apartments equipped as a laboratory. His sinister assistants were known as the Magi.

Alchemy was essentially the pointless pursuit of trying to turn base metal into gold. Through the experimental processes however a great deal was learned about the properties of metals and chemical compounds. Scientific information was faithfully recorded.

Even within the context of the times though Henry was regarded as an eccentric. His response to this was to encourage the superstition and fear. It encouraged people to leave him alone.

During the year 1614 three workers at the castle died in mysterious circumstances. One had apparently committed suicide by throwing himself down a well. Another had suffered convulsions and had fallen from the battlements. A third apparently choked to death on nothing more dangerous than a fish bone.

In public opinion the ninth earl was responsible for these events. Henry couldn't care less what people thought. He hid himself away in the lab and carried on with his experiments. Finally after years of failure he could stand no more. He dismissed the Magi, tore down the lab and took up more traditional lordly pursuits.

Henry made up for lost time in rapidly earning a reputation for drunkenness and debauchery that was second to none. This of course was much more acceptable in the public eye. Henry the Wizard became Henry the Red Nosed. It was a kind of rehabilitation.

Former Glories

Alnwick Castle is inextricably linked to the Earls and Dukes of Northumberland. Until the 16th. century Warkworth remained the favoured Percy stronghold. It was the first of the present line of Dukes who reversed that preference. Since that time Warkworth's decline has been more than matched by the growth and influence of Alnwick.

The history of Alnwick Castle and the Percys in particular is well documented elsewhere in this series.*

Keeping His Head

But one important Earl has been previously overlooked.

The 6th. Earl, Henry Algernon, fell deeply in love with the young Anne Boleyn. When Henry VIII also became infatuated with her, the Earl knew it was time to call off the contest.

But the association remained important. When King Henry tired of his second wife he tried to persuade the Earl that he had made a promise and pre-contract to marry her. He also tried to coerce the Earl to admit that he had been the queen's lover.

Either of these would have been enough to condemn the queen. The admission of the pre-contract would have been particularly helpful to the king in securing an annulment. The second would have damaged the queen's reputation - a precedent assumed that Anne was a virgin bride. The Earl did his best to save her. He took an oath before both archbishops to say there had been no promise, no contract, and no sex.

This made life more difficult for the king. It has been argued that if Henry Algernon had done as he was told the break with Rome would not have been necessary.

As they say, the rest is history. The Earl survived but the consequences for the family were considerable. Henry Algernon had no direct heir. His nephew, Thomas Percy, was temporarily deprived of the inheritance by an attainder put on his father for taking part in the Pilgrimage of Grace.

The Earl's gesture was also futile. King Henry had Anne Boleyn beheaded after she was found guilty of charges of adultery and incest.

Where Shepherds' Rest

Leave Alnwick by the Clayport Bank - the B6341 road to Rothbury.

Close to the apex of the hill is the excellent Shepherd's Rest hostelry. A nearby green was once a noted meeting place for fairies.

The B6341 runs below Corby Crags with fine views to the Cheviots in the north.

Just below the high moor Edlingham Castle can be seen to the right below. Turn onto the narrow road and cross the stream.

Unknown Identity

On a summers morning three centuries ago a courting couple walking beside the stream made a grisly discovery.

They came across the bodies of two young women with their heads submerged in the water. It was evident that drowning was the method of murder. The bodies were joined together at the wrist by a knotted leather strip.

Nobody recognised the dead women and the motive for the crime was unknown. Their features however were very similar. It is likely they were sisters close in age, or even twins. Their clothing and jewellery was of gipsy style.

At that time it was the habit of the gipsies to hold their own courts. Death by drowning was a sentence passed on women who committed adultery with 'outsiders' or the menfolk of a rival family. The tieing at the wrists was symbolic : it suggested that the two women were regarded as partners in crime.

Even this is mainly supposition. What really happened is now unlikely to be ever discovered.

Ancient Walls

Park by the church of St. John the Baptist. This is one of the oldest continuously used Christian sites in Northumbria.

Part of the first stone building, dating from around 1050, can still be identified in the nave. As early as AD 737 King Ceowulf gave this land to the monks of Lindisfarne. It is likely that some sort of wooden chapel was built soon

St. John The Baptist, Edlingham

afterwards. An Anglo-Saxon church is said to have been consecrated here by Bishop Egred in AD 840.

The most notable feature today is the weather-beaten 12th. century doorway. There is a 14th. century grave cover in front of the entrance. The carving is of the sword and the shears - powerful symbols of the borderers' way of life. The 14th. century west tower has narrow slit windows which suggests the building had a defensive as a well as a religious part to play during the age of the reivers.

The Witch Trial

The unusual low lying Edlingham Castle is essentially a fortified manor house dating from the 12th. century. For many years this was the property of the Swinburne family.

There is a stile in the wall by the church that leads to the ruined castle.

In 1682 the Swinburne agent, John Mills, claimed that he was plagued by a witch called Margaret Stothard. In his evidence to the magistrate, Mills declared :

Edlingham Castle

" Lying awake one Sunday night I did hear a great blast of wind. Immediately following something fell like a great weight on my heart. It gave a cry like a cat and then another in the same manner. When this was ended there appeared a light at the end of the bed, and in this light I did recognise Margaret Stothard. For a time my speech was taken from me. When I'd recovered the power to speak I cried out ' the Witch, the Witch! '"

" On another night I was so frightened that the hairs of my head did stand on end. I had to leap from my bed to take up the reading of my bible before I was calm again. "

Another witness was William Collingwood. He claimed he knew of a case when Margaret Stothard had been called to cure a sick child. This was apparently achieved by sucking the breath from the child's mouth. This reversed artificial respiration seems to have aided the youngster's recovery. According to

Collingwood however the cure was achieved at a price. A goat tied up outside the building went berserk and had to be slaughtered.

Another story was told by Jacob Mills. This time Margaret Stothard had waved a cloth over a sick baby. When the infant died some days later there was little doubt as to who was responsible.

Isabel Maine was another witness. She claimed to have consulted Margaret Stothard when the cows produced sour milk. The suggested remedy of using a scrubbing solution of salt and water seemed to work. Butter and cheese were soon back in full production. Quite what Isabel had to complain about is unclear.

Despite this welter of 'evidence' the trial ended without a verdict. Margaret Stothard died peacefully in her bed.

𝕿𝖍𝖊 𝕳𝖎𝖌𝖍𝖜𝖆𝖞 𝕳𝖆𝖚𝖓𝖙𝖎𝖓𝖌

Where the Rothbury road crosses the A 697 a clump of trees can be seen on a small rise to the left.

The ghost of an highwayman is said to haunt this area. Certainly there have been many reports of a 'strange oppressive atmosphere' sensed particularly by animals.

The late Reverend Jack Richardson**, the most famous of modern Northumbrian ghosthunters, searched for evidence of a phantom coach and horses around this spot. The link between the coach and highwayman has never been firmly established but it is a credible one.

An incident that occurred in the late 17th. century offers something towards a possible explanation.

What began as a routine robbery ended in tragedy when a coach and six were halted by two highway robbers near this junction. One of the passengers had a concealed pistol which he carelessly discharged. It was a fellow passenger, not one of the robbers, who was slightly wounded.

More importantly, the explosion caused the horses to bolt. The coachman had already dismounted. He stood with the robbers watching the coach disappear into the distance. The passengers were helpless.

The coach was found in a ditch. Two of the passengers escaped with minor injuries. A third - the wounded man - suffered a blow to the head which left him permanently ' enfeebled in the brain.'

The last passenger was a young woman who delivered a stillborn child some hours later.

Lord Armstrong's Masterpiece

A quarter of a million people each year come to enjoy the estate and grounds at Cragside.

The property, which is in the care of the National Trust, is well worth a visit. It reflects the considerable vision of Victorian entrepreneur, Lord Armstrong, who created something wonderful from what was little more than moorland.*

Opposite the official entrance, which is by no means the only one used by visitors, there is a signpost to Debdon. Park before the first gate.

Fairies And Witches

Shortly beyond the gate the road divides. Both options make pleasant enough walks.

The lower path runs past Primrose Cottage once associated with a local coven. The upper path leads to Debdon Farm. A nearby field has been variously described as the place of the sabbat and the dancing green of the fairies.

This truly is a place where the visitor can decide between the right and left hand paths...

* See Ghost Trails of Northumbria
** See More Ghost Trails of Northumbria

No. 3
Around The Tyne Valley

This linear tour takes about five hours

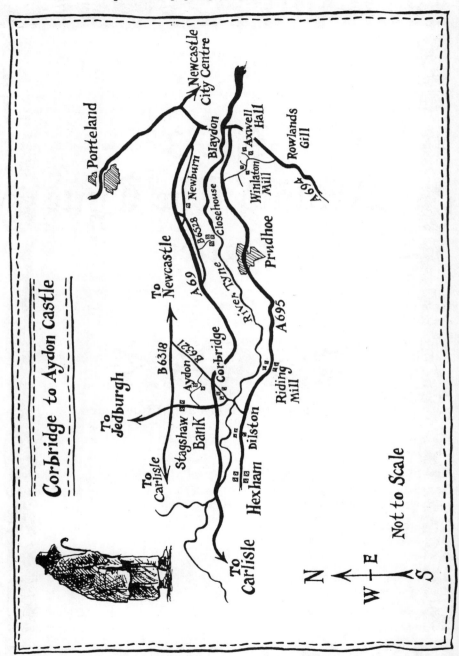

Corbridge to Aydon Castle

Not to Scale

A Wide Variety

The Tyne Valley is often neglected by visitors to Northumbria, yet there is nowhere in the area that contains such a variety of interest and scenery.

Start at Stagshaw Bank on the A68 just outside Corbridge. You will see the dark silhouetted shape of Stagshaw church and minor roads leading off to Aydon, Halton and Sandhoe.

The Famous Fair

The fair held here annually from 1204 until 1927 was so famous that it attracted people from all round the country. At its peak in the 13th. and 14th. centuries it has been estimated that up to 25,000 people attended - a staggering figure given the much thinner population of late medieval period.

There was wheeling and dealing certainly. Second hand cart salesman did the medieval equivalent of clocking vehicles by covering up worn joints and axles with heavy layers of goose fat. Quacks made outrageous medicinal claims for coloured water, and the relics of saints were common currency.

But the fair was primarily a social occasion. People met people. There was dancing, pageantry, and competition. The best wrestlers, finest archers, and sweetest singers all came to Stagshaw.

Much Trouble At The Fair

There is some evidence that Robin Hood was a native of Redesdale.** This perhaps lends tentative support to the story of Mutch the Miller's murder at Stagshaw.

According to folklore, some of the Merrie Men continued in the wealth recycling business long after the death of their leader. This caused them to be outlawed for a second time after the accession of King John.

The price on the heads of such noted outlaws was high. One tradition has Little John and Will Scarlett escaping to the semi-safe haven of William the Lion's Scotland. Friar Tuck returned to a friary.

The same tradition has Miller - whose regular bolthole is unknown - visiting the Stagshaw fair.

The world's oldest profession was also well represented. After sampling rather too much of one of the heady brews, the outlaw decided to show one of these young women his name was no exaggeration of the truth.

Unhappily the booze had loosened his tongue as much as his trousers. He carelessly revealed his identity.

The woman realised that Mutch was potentially a far more valuable transaction than she'd imagined. The death of the miller could earn her a lot of dough.

At an opportune moment she took a long pin from her kirtle and thrust it deep into his chest. The point pierced his heart and within seconds he was dead. The news of the murder spread quickly around the fair. An angry crowd soon turned on the woman. She was tied to a tree and used for archery practice.

An Ancient And Modern Problem

The least delightful aspect of a summer visit to Corbridge is the parking problem. But this has been a busy town since the Romans recognised its strategic importance as a Tyne crossing place. It is possible to imagine the chaos caused by double parked chariots two millenniums ago.

Two important Roman roads - Dere Street and the Stanegate - intersected here.

A Capital Place

Parking apart, Corbridge is a capital place to visit. Once the capital of all Northumbria it has now been demoted to capital of the Tynedale District.

International Incidents

When King Ethelred of Northumbria was murdered here in AD 796, the Emperor Charlemagne hastily created an alliance between the Kingdom of Northumbria and the Kingdom of the Franks.

A professional Viking rape and pillager, Ragnald, took on a combined army at Corbridge in AD 918. His victory led to the establishment of a Danish kingdom the following year. When Ragnald chose York for his capital this signalled the decline in importance of Corbridge.

King David I of Scotland occupied the town in 1138. It was part of a campaign to detach Northumbria and Cumbria from the rest of King Stephen's anarchic English kingdom. The fact that he was unsuccessful has been a cause of regret to many northerners ever since.

Growth And Decline

By late medieval times Corbridge had again become a prosperous town. Despite regular unwelcome attention from border raiders and three equally devastating visits from King John, its growing prosperit seemed assured.

But one force was too much for Corbridge to stand. The town was attacked by bubonic plague. Estimates suggest that up to two thirds of the population was carried off by this scourge. For several centuries afterwards Corbridge was little more than a village. Recovery was slow but accelerated in the 18th. and 19th. centuries.

Today the town is a small gem. It has a pleasingly leafy open aspect that compliments a sense of historical importance.

Echoes Of The Past

St. Andrews Church echoes this history. It is one of the most important Saxon churches in Northumbria. Part of the lower tower dates from the eighth century or earlier. The round tower arch inside is a former Roman gateway imported from nearby Corstopitum. Part of one window is distinctly Saxon. The south doorway features Norman zigzag work but most of the interior is 13th. century.

The Vicar's Pele, Corbridge

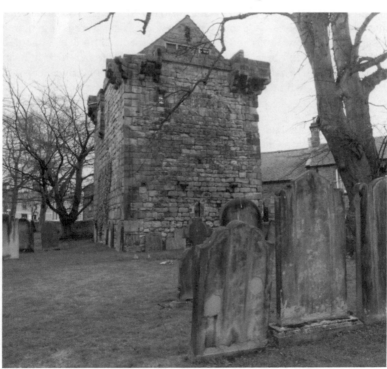

The Vicar's pele tower is set at the edge of the churchyard. The middle floor was designed for human habitation. At times of danger cattle were rounded up into the basement. The upper floor was important for defence.

John Stearne's Visit

John Stearne, assistant to the notorious witchfinder, Matthew Hopkins, came to Corbridge in 1652.

His mission was to 'secure confessions of those tainted by witchery'. There are no records of his success or otherwise, but trials by pricking were almost certainly held in the market place. A similar scene was recalled by a contemporary writer when a witchfinder set about his work in Morpeth.**

A Murder Mystery

The body of a young woman was found on common ground near the town in 1583.

In what was almost a prototype attack for the 19th. century London Ripper, a serious attempt had been made to disembowel her. There were a large number of more superficial stab wounds and it is likely that she had also been strangled. Her ears and part of her left breast had been cut off and placed in a bloody heap next to the rest of her. What remained was a scarcely recognisable heap of flesh twisted awkwardly with the legs and arms folded around the torso.

The sign of the cross had been cut into her forehead.

The young woman had been the daughter of a Corbridge innkeeper, who carried on a successful business of her own in an upper room. Her popularity with both visitors and locals - male of course- had made her something of a celebrity. The manner of her death caused outrage.

On the evening before the body was found, witnesses had seen her talking to a tall distinguished looking man in clerical garb. Some said that she had later invited him to her upstairs sanctum, others that they had left the inn together.

The man was never seen again. Other murderous attacks on prostitutes - at Carlisle and Penrith - occurred weeks before the Corbridge murder. In each case the women were stabbed and strangled and the corpses were marked by the carving of the cross on the forehead. What was distinctly different about the Cumbrian cases is that there was no further mutilation.

The theory of a deranged religious zealot taking a terrible revenge on fallen women has been suggested. This is not entirely satisfactory. There are no clues as to the identity of the Carlisle killer, but in Penrith the finger of suspicion was pointed at a recruiting officer who had been in the town some time. He too disappeared on the day the crime was discovered.

Attempts have been made to link the Corbridge murder with other violent deaths in the region at around the same time. Again this has been unsatisfactory largely because accurate records of events at the end of the 16th. century are patchy and heavily pinned on secondary sources. The identity and motive of the Corbridge killer is likely to remain in the mystery file.

The Ruins of Dilston Castle

The Dilston Ghost

Cross the Tyne Bridge and turn right towards the Hexham Road. After a short way turn left towards Blanchland. The ruined castle tower can be clearly seen through the trees.

This was once the home of James Radcliffe, the last Earl of Derwentwater. James was persuaded by his wife to join the doomed Stuart cause in 1715.* On the night before his execution the Aurora Borealis shone brilliantly in the sky

41

over the Tyne. This was taken as a portent and the Northern Lights were placed in local folklore as Lord Derwentwater's Lights.

There was a terrible storm on the morning of the execution. One account says the hall gutters ran red with blood. Even less likely are the reports of thousands of adders - never seen before - swimming in the Tyne. Each of these is taken to represent the soul of one of James Radcliffe's fallen followers. There are few limits to the imagination of country folk.

Certainly it was a messy execution. James Radcliffe was customarily generous to his executioner, but the axeman did not repay him with an efficient dispatch. The first blow was aimed too low and failed to sever the neck. The second over compensated and struck the base of the skull. Although the earl would have been insensible by this stage it required a lusty third strike to complete the task.

His embalmed body was brought back to Dilston and laid in the small chapel close to the hall. The ghost is most frequently spotted wandering in the woods by nearby Devil's Water. As this is a premier league phantom, featuring the traditional grisly severed head, an encounter is not recommended.

A strange ghostly light sometimes seen shining from the ruined Dilston Tower is said to be a beacon placed there to guide his spirit home.

Devil's Water

The castle stands amongst mature trees above Devil's Water. The name conjures up a popular misinterpretation. It derives from the Norman holders of the barony - the d'Eivills.

The family may have been sensitive about sound association. The name was Anglicised to Dyvelston. The considerable foundations of the d'Eivill fortress were uncovered during 19th. century excavations. They are close to walls of the present castle.

Where the ground slopes down to the river the remains of two underground passages were discovered. One of these probably linked with an underground room from which steps were cut through the rock to stream level.

Hot From The Coven

Turn right on the A695 for Riding Mill. There are excellent views over the Tyne Valley from the road.

Riding Mill - particularly the area around the Wellington Hotel - is associated with a large 17th. century coven of witches.

It is said that a member of the coven suffered a bizarre punishment for telling trade secrets. She was stripped and tied to a large oak table and seven candles were secured to a bracket above her. For several hours the hot wax was allowed to drip onto her. Then the wax was scraped away, re-heated, and used to seal her mouth.

The woman survived this ordeal but died a month later of pneumonia.

A Famous Stronghold

Continue on the A695 to Prudhoe. Turn left at the traffic lights towards the industrial estate. The castle is signposted. The final bank is so steep it should only be attempted by light vehicles.

The castle, now in the care of English Heritage, dates from the reign of Henry I.

Shortly after the conquest King William ' rewarded' his most valued follower with the Barony of Redesdale. This first Baron Umfraville - the splendidly named Robin with the Beard - was also given William's sword and charged to ' defend himself against wolves and the king's enemies.'

At a later date the barony was added to the other Umfraville possessions. The Castle was begun by Odinel de Umfraville who had refused to acknowledge the claim of William the Lion of Scotland to Northumberland.

When the Lion invaded, one of his first objectives was Prudhoe. The siege failed but the Lion returned for a second bite the following year. This time Odinel had reinforcements from York and the Lion was forced to roar off in a northerly direction. Odinel fully earned his reputation as a Lion tamer. He was even in on the act when King William was captured at Alnwick.

Later Umfravilles accompanied Richard I on his crusade, and stood beside Edward II at Bannockburn.

The castle passed to the Percys in the 14th. century.

It is now a noble ruin, but sufficiently well preserved to create an impression of invincibility. Apart from Norham, the keep is the oldest in the county.

An Unusual Haunting

One of Prudhoe's many ghosts may hold the key to an unsolved murder. On the warmer days of the year, at around sunset, a ghostly figure has been seen wandering the grounds.

The spectre is that of a woman dressed in the full finery of early Tudor gentry. The wraith appears to be in some distress as she walks to a particular spot and pauses before pointing towards the ground.

The performance has been repeated so many times it's possible to locate the spot fairly accurately. Although even the foundations are covered, the spectre is clearly at the site of the Great Hall.

Will excavations one day reveal a secret that has been buried for centuries?

Jackie Brown And The Blaydon Burn

Follow the A695 towards Blaydon. Avoid the first Blaydon turning and keep to the upper road. Follow the signposted route to Blaydon Burn, Winlanton and Winlanton Mill.

Jackie Brown, the former verger of St. Cuthbert's Parish Church, was quite a character.

His friend, Geordie Riley, who wrote the regional anthem 'Blaydon Races', gave Jackie a kind of immortality by including his name in the song. Jackie deserves this. He was a great music hall fan who organised regular 'cultural' trips for local people. He was also a self appointed town crier and master of ceremonies at events around Blaydon.

He is perhaps remembered most fondly for his work with young people. Years before youth leaders were invented, Jackie organised parties, picnics, and trips to the countryside.

His ghost, a benign spirit no doubt, is said to haunt the Blaydon Burn.

Suicide Spot

Letch Wood to the south of Winlanton is a famous suicide spot. Many of the old beech branches have proved accessible and reliable for the purpose.

It is a bleak and desolate place that would do little to encourage cheerful thoughts. Locals have said that walking around here is sufficient in itself to provoke a fit of depression. It is therefore not recommended as a picnic place.

The most celebrated suicide occurred in 1660. The man who was charged with reading the Restoration Proclamation killed himself a few hours later. This is said to be connected with part of the document that said there would be no pardon for the regicides - those who signed the death warrant of Charles I.

The man was buried at the nearby Four Lane Ends. A stake was drilled through his heart.

This is a section of the local 'Corpse Road' which runs from the old mill to the churchyards at Ryton. All local inhabitants made their final journey along this road.

In Northumbria, only Chillingham Castle* offers a greater local concentration of spooky stories. It seems that every old building comes fully furnished with its own ghostly ensemble.

Derwent Valley Country Park

At the junction of Thornley Lane and the A694 turn left. The road follows alongside the Derwent Valley Country Park - an excellent place to take a respite from a hard day's Murder Trailing.

A Halloween Special

The people of Winlanton Mill know how to celebrate halloween in style. Perhaps this is based on a long local tradition of witchery.

Centuries ago the notorious Scot's witch, Isobel Gowdie, brought her ' black ministry' to Winlanton. This is reputed to have given the local coven special powers. Certainly it created a special local enthusiasm for dark deeds.

The 'ordained' head witch of Winlanton was called Suva. Her followers had the measure of dedication that is created through fear.

Goats, sheep, and even dogs were found with their throats slit and innards removed. Dreadful curses were put on those who threatened the coven.

Coven Fresh

Beyond this we move into the spectrum of wild and improbable stories. It is said that Queen Suva was seen as some kind of demon goddess. Her cookery book included recipes for rats, slugs, lice, spiders and the occasional fresh corpse. The cadaver of a child - the younger the better - was a particularly tasty ingredient. In the finest gastronomic traditions nothing was ever wasted: unused limbs and organs were stored in jars.

Queen Suva was said to use any method necessary to collect her ingredients. Far from stopping at murder, it was often the first instruction on the recipe sheet.

There is speculation that the coven is alive and well today. Certainly there are those around Winlanton Mill who will tell you so. But visitors asking too many questions are not encouraged to hang around. Journalists, writers and researchers are made to feel as welcome as a winter virus.

It all adds up to a feeling that there may just be more to the Winlanton coven than can be found on the dusty pages of history.

Axwell Hall

Axwell Hall is signposted off the A694. It has now fallen to ruin, but it's an imposing gothic building set in a rural oasis. The hall was built in the late 18th. century as the residence of the Member if Parliament for Durham. It is forever linked with the name of the Clavering family.

In a later incarnation the building was used as a reform school. It was closed in 1981.

In many ways the youngsters at the school had better lives than those in the surrounding mining communities. Durham pit owners were famous for their exploitation of both child and female labour. These unfortunate folk were readily employed because their wages were so much lower than those of the men. Long hours underground took their toll. Life expectancy was about 44 years. This figure partly reflects the unwillingness of the owners to introduce 'uneconomic' safety measures.

Timely Justice

A noted local murder is placed around three centuries earlier.

The story goes that a young country squire had taken a fancy to a young lady who worked in his household. Although she at first rejected his advances, he made her such promises that finally she succumbed.

Soon she was pregnant and sent away from the hall to avoid the taint of scandal. The squire promised to 'look after her' but soon found himself a new mistress. The old one now faced poverty and hunger.

The rejected women returned to Axwell with a baby boy in her arms. She confronted the man with his fecklessness and promised to tell all if she was not properly recompensed.

He agreed to meet her the following week with some valuable jewels as her payoff. The meeting took place at night in a wooded area close to the dene at Blaydon. The next day the strangled woman was found by a forester. The baby, lying nearby, was close to death from exposure. The man took the infant to his cottage.

There were rumours and no doubt one or two people guessed at the truth. But the squire was too influential a figure to be brought to justice.

He returned to his favourite country pursuits - hunting, drinking and debauchery. As time went by his taste for old port and ever younger women accelerated the pace of dissipation.

18 years passed. The young squire was now prematurely old and unsteady in his walk. But against advice he continued to ride with the hounds.

An accident was inevitable. On the fateful day he fell behind the field, then more heavily from his horse.

The young forester who found him carried the considerable bulk on his sturdy shoulders. But the squire's weight would have challenged a sumo wrestler. As he came close to the cottage he called out to his father for assistance.

The squire was now regaining consciousness and squealing with the pain of his broken legs. He appealed to the two men for their further assistance.

The older forester did not at first recognise the much altered squire. But when he spoke his name, memories came flooding back. It had taken a long time, but now was the hour of justice.

The older forester introduced the squire to the 'baby' he had left to perish in the cold. He had now become the sturdy youth who had found the injured man in the forest.

The squire begged for mercy and the two men promised not harm him. He was however invited to find his own way home. The squire crawled for almost half a mile before his body could no longer stand the pain inflicted on it.

It is said that not one of his workers, or any person from the locality, attended the funeral.

A Change Of Character

Blaydon's modern shopping precinct is a soulless place. Even without the graffiti and wind-swept crisp packets it would still somehow look untidy.

The contrast is even more marked because of the style of houses and shops in the adjacent streets. This was not the golden age of architecture either but there is a dignity and solid feel about it all. You have the feeling it will survive after the new precinct has been swept away by the bulldozers.

The Music Man

The old Empire Building, known as the Electric Theatre and later Woolworths, had a rather unusual ghost.

It seems that a former pianist returned long after he had exchanged his piano for a harp. He had played for years in a pit under the screen.

Nobody ever saw the hands that played the keys but the style was distinctive. What is more, the old piano had a dud upper B flat so tunes were transposed to avoid this.

Even 40 years later snatches of popular music hall tunes and the rumbling cadences of film accompaniments were occasionally heard in the vicinity. The theatre had by then become a bingo hall.

When Buster And Charlie Reigned

The Electric Theatre had its heyday in the era of silent film. Later there were popular children's Saturday matinees and the 'latest' feature films for adults in the evenings. Cinemas in the 40's and 50's often held a 'standby film' in case the programmed movie was not delivered. At the Electric Theatre the 'standby' for almost two decades was 'The Charge at Feather River'. It is said that the people of Blaydon knew the dialogue - such as it was - by heart.

Death Of A Deputy

Blaydon Dene is at the eastern end of the town. The famous Old Hazard colliery was nearby.

A pit deputy died here in mysterious circumstances. The official view was that he had accidentally got caught up in some winding gear and had suffered fatal injuries.

At the time of the incident is was widely whispered he had been pushed to his death. The man had been enormously unpopular. It is suggested that a murder enquiry would have been pointless - there were 150 likely assassins.

Passion In A Puddle

Follow the north bank of the Tyne to Newburn. The hall - a red brick three story building on the left - is now an old peoples' home. There is a clock above the conservatory frontage.

The original Newburn Hall, that stood nearby, was built in the 15th. century. It was cleared to make way for a steelworks extension.

Several centuries ago a young man called Frankie Johnson worked as a groom in the stables.

His passion for a housemaid was revealed when the two of them were caught in bed together. The traditions of the time meant one of them had to go. Ordinarily the maid would been seen as more readily dispensable, but she had become a favourite of the mistress, so it was Frankie who was given his 'cards'.

But this misfortune was not enough to dampen the ardour of the young lovers. Even when Frankie's new job took him across the river they met whenever they could.

Most of their assignations were at night. His lodgings were in a house opposite Newburn Hall. He would light a candle in his bedroom window as a signal. She would climb from her own window and rush down to the river bank. He would wade and swim across. Finally they would enjoy an embrace that was as passionate as it was moist.

But Frankie's wet wanderings were also courting disaster. One autumn evening the flow was just too strong for him and he floated off towards Tynemouth. The body was not recovered but loud screams from the river have caused many an alarm over the years.

Close House

At Newburn these are largely ignored.

" It's jus' wor Frankie, " they say.

Coining It In

Pass the section of Hadrian's Wall at Heddon and take the B6528 to Horsley.

The old Lion and Lamb pub is worth a pit stop. It offers good beer and food in a pleasant atmosphere. This hostelry is also said to feature the ghost of an avaricious Victorian landlord. The manifestation does not seem to go beyond the sound of jangling coins, but it is nevertheless disconcerting when the lounge is empty.

The Researchers

Turn left off the B6528 for Close House. Then turn left and left again.

Close House, splendidly surrounded by mature trees, is now a major outdoor recreation centre. The stable buildings rival the house itself for symmetry and style.

This was once the focal point of another coven. This particular group are best remembered for their experiments with the whiter shades of witchery.

They used distillations and suffusions of flowers, berries, and herbs. Claims were made for the power of these remedies against ailments as varied as dysentery, gout, and impotence. Today we would probably call it alternative medicine.

There is no historical link between 'research' carried out round here in the present and past. It is nevertheless a pleasing coincidence to note that the fields around Close House are agricultural test beds for Newcastle University.

The Fall Of The Wolf

The splendidly named Ethelwald Moll, who was briefly king of Northumbria in the 8th. century, was responsible for the death of one of his vassals who held this land.

This man, Raedwulf, had formed an attachment to the king's sister. Through the misty mirror of more than twelve centuries it is difficult to be sure of exactly why the king disapproved. It is not unlikely however that Raedwulf and the king's sister were planning a takeover bid for Ethelwald's throne.

The king sent some of his henchmen to find Raedwulf who prudently decided to lie low. Ethelwald's next tactic was more subtle. He started a rumour that his sister was sick, and made sure it would be believed by arranging for her to be systematically poisoned.

This brought Raedwulf running. The king showed dutiful concern for his sister by allowing Raedwulf to be at her bedside as she expired. But as he left the death chamber he was met by two of Ethelwald's larger lads.

They insulted the memory of the dead woman. Raedwulf was suitably provoked and swords were drawn. Raedwulf gave a pretty good account of himself until one of his assailants shortened the odds by drawing a dagger.

As Raedwulf protected himself against a succession of blows aimed at his skull, he was unable to prevent the dagger being thrust into his stomach. Raedwulf collapsed. His assailants, who were naturally impatient after waiting so long for the king's sister to die, decided to finish the job immediately. They cut off his head.

Ethelwald made a public display of grief when he heard of the two deaths. The performance would have been all the more convincing if he hadn't followed it by rewarding Raedwulf's killers with gifts of land.

But nobody was likely to be fooled. The art of Northumbrian kingship was survival. Removing Raedwulf had become politically expedient. Those who implemented the king's 'policy' earned his gratitude.

It is almost a model for modern cabinet government.

An Expensive Mistake

Go to the A69 and travel westwards. The fragmentary ruin of Nafferton Castle is just visible over the east bound carriageway from a lay-by.

The castle evokes a bitter conflict between two Northumbrian warlords. Today we would call it a row about planning permission.

It was begun by Philip de Ulecote, Forester of Northumberland, who was a favourite of King John. Although it was against the law to create such a stronghold without the king's approval, Philip was able to take this for granted.

But Richard de Umfraville, Lord of Prudhoe, took exception to this building work so close to his own power base. After John's death he petitioned the new king - Henry III - and Philip de Ulecote was forced to stop the work.

The Sheriff of the County was given orders to remove the timber and a brattice tower. This was taken to Newcastle and used to improve fortifications there.

Philip de Ulecote was not a happy man. He promptly brought it to the king's attention that the second Umfraville castle - at Harbottle** - was also an 'adulterine', or illegal stronghold.

The king had to agree and royal letters ordered the destruction of Harbottle. It is doubtful that this was implemented. At the end of the same century Harbottle was still strong enough to withstand a besieging force of 40,000 men.

But Nafferton too earned a unique place in Northumbrian history. It was the only castle that was ruined before it was built, and the site has never been returned to for further construction.

Murder At Melton

But the half finished keep is remembered for something else. It later become the lair of the notorious villain, Lang Lonkin. He was a robber, ruffian, and murderer on a grand scale who terrorised the district for more than 20 years.

His most famous crime took place at Welton Hall.

Lang Lonkin was admitted by a servant called Orange with a grievance against the absent Lord of Welton.

A ballad of the time includes these verses :

" ' Where's the Ladies of the hall? ' Says the Lonkin ; ' They're up in their chambers,' Says Orange to him. ' How shall we get them down?' Says the Lonkin ; 'Prick the baby in the cradle.' Says Orange to him."

The ballad goes on to describe how the young mother rushed downstairs when she hears the baby crying. He killed the child first and then the mother before throwing the bodies into a hole still indicated on the map a 'Lang Lonkin's Hole.'

He escaped justice for this crime. Although his lair was well known it is said that he concealed himself in a secret tunnel linking the castle with the nearby Nafferton Farm.

Lang Lonkin later became deranged and hung himself from a tree close to the castle. His skull was placed on a stone within the walls. It stayed there untouched for many years and remained the focus of local fear and superstition.

'Lunkin' passed into local speech as an alternative to bogeyman. Children were warned that if they strayed for from home, especially after nightfall, that Lunkin would get them.

The Road To Aydon

Take the B6530 towards Corbridge from the A69, then turn first right towards Aydon. At Aydon village turn right again then left. The castle is signposted as one mile but this is an optimistic estimate.

Follow the burn to the castle. Continuing along the same road will eventually return you to Stagshaw Bank.

There is access to the scenic gorge below via a steep path beyond the castle.

Aydon Castle

Jock's Leap

A gang of moss troopers were captured on a raid lead by Sir Robert Clavering. His arbitrary justice was to have them thrown into the gorge. Just one of them managed to escape by leaping across the river. The spot where this happened is still called 'Jock's Leap'.

Well Worth A Visit

The castle is essentially a fortified manor house that was begun in 1296.

It is one of the best preserved small castles in Northumbria. The defences in particular are still more or less complete. A great deal of preservation work has been carried out in recent years.

The stages of development can still be traced. The original modest manor house of the Aydons was fortified by Robert de Raymes in the early part of the 14th. century. A sturdy outer wall encloses three courtyards with the main buildings, which include the great hall, at the centre.

But Aydon does more than represent the past. It's a time capsule that captures the mood of history. A visit is highly recommended.

* See Ghost Trails of Northumbria
** See More Ghost Trails of   Northumbria

No. 4
Berwick-Upon-Tweed

This circular walking tour takes about three hours

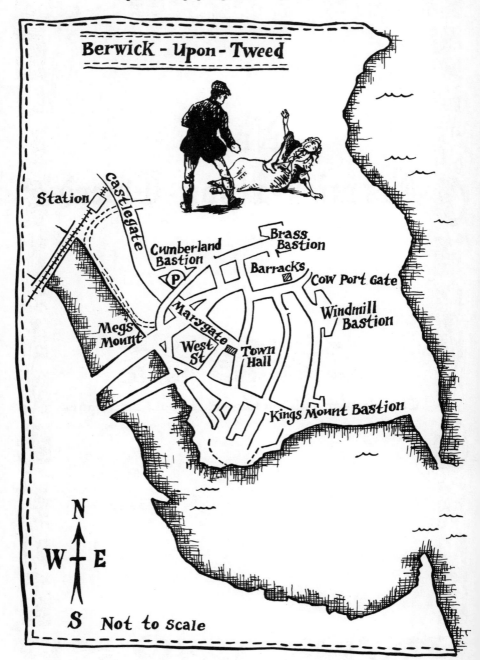

Berwick - Upon - Tweed

Station

Castlegate

Cumberland Bastion

Brass Bastion

P

Barracks

Cow Port Gate

Megs Mount

Marygate

Windmill Bastion

West St

Town Hall

Kings Mount Bastion

N
W E
S Not to scale

Bonnie Berwick

Berwick-upon-Tweed is not as popular with visitors as it deserves to be. A visit to Northumbria without a visit to Berwick is like going to Egypt and missing the pyramids.

The walled town, spectacularly set close to the mouth of the Tweed, has many unique historical features. No other town in Britain has experienced such a turbulent history.

A Brief History

King Ida of Bernicia, the first acknowledged ruler of this northern part of Northumbria, based his kingdom at Bamburgh.* By the time the kingdom was united under Ecgfrith more than a century later (in AD 670) Berwick was well established as part of the northern frontier. It was assimilated into the new English kingdom early in the tenth century.

Around 110 years later - in 1018 - Berwick was claimed 'for Scotland by King Malcolm II after his success at the Battle of Carham'. It was from this time that the town began to develop as a port. It was lost back to the English crown after the retreat of William the Lion in 1174.

From that date, almost until modern times, Berwick has lead a chequered existence.

Richard the Lionheart sold the Scots their independence to raise money. King John visited the town and committed atrocities that were barbaric even by the standards of the time.

But it was during this late medieval era that the town reached its zenith in prestige an importance. One contemporary account claims Berwick matched Alexandria as a city of merchant princes. Although this was probably more public relations than reality, it shows that the merchants of Berwick had already discovered that it pays to advertise.

Edward I took the part of John Baliol against Robert the Bruce, and in controversial circumstances awarded him the throne north of the border. Then the English king undermined Baliol's position by treating him as a subject.

Berwick showed what it thought of all this by becoming the first town to sign the Treaty of Revolt.

The price paid for the initiative was a terrible one. Edward I reduced the 'glorious seaport of the north' to ashes. Its trading importance disappeared overnight. It has never again approached such a position of ascendancy.

In order to defend his position the English king ordered new walls to defend the town.

Robert the Bruce's attempt to take it back in 1312 was thwarted by the barking of a dog. Edward II fled here after his defeat at Bannockburn two years later. In 1318 Robert the Bruce made a second and successful attempt to capture it.

The English failed to win it back the following year, and finally bowed to Scottish supremacy after further humiliations in 1322. Robert the Bruce died in 1327 after signing the treaty that recognised him as king of an independent nation.

But the peaceful era for Berwick was short lived. In 1333 it returned to England after the Battle of Halidon Hill. A century later Henry VI handed it back during the Wars of the Roses. It was finally regained for England in 1482 and created a free burgh under Edward IV's treaty.

This semi independent status was something that the people of Berwick enjoyed greatly. There is something of this in the town even today although the status was officially lost under the Reform Act of 1885.

Even during the Jacobite risings, when Berwick was very much a Hanoverian base, the locals continued to assert their independence.

In 1746 an attempt was made to force conformity. The Wales and Berwick Act stated :

' that in all cases where the Kingdom of England, or that part of England called England, hath been or shall be mentioned in any Act of Parliament, the name has been and shall henceforth be declared and taken to include the Dominion of Wales and the Town of Berwick-upon-Tweed.'

This Act failed to impress the locals. At the end of the Crimean War they refused to sign the peace treaty with Russia, and remained technically at war until the final conciliatory days of the communist era.

An Independent Spirit

In many ways the independent spirit of Berwick remains. Their Rangers football team have been long established in the Scottish league. Rivalry between Berwickers and gangs from north of the border causes occasional headaches for the two constabularies. Professional poaching and illegal netting still boost the town's economy.

This is not to paint a picture of Berwick as a sort of Wild West frontier town. The people have a reputation for straightforwardness and honesty, especially in dealings with each other and with outsiders. It's just that the rules in this unique place seem to be slightly different...

Where Culture And Fun Combine

The local accent mixes the throatiness of the lowland Scots with the accentuated vowel sounds of the Northumbrian. It has been described by an commentator on linguistic networks 'as a delightful assault on the ears'.

Berwick has a vigorous culture of its own too. The Maltings Arts Centre reflects this in regular exhibitions. The centre also provides the best and most varied programme of musical and theatrical events in the region. There is an art gallery and several museums. The range of entertainments, and sports and leisure facilities, is remarkable in such a small town.

The Phantom Train

Park in the large car park beyond the Gateway Hypermarket. Turn right into Castlegate, the left for Railway Street after the Post Office. Once inside the station building follow the stairs up and down to the platform area.

The locals delight in telling the tale of the phantom train. As the story progresses it becomes clear that the train is only supernatural in the sense that it arrives at the time published in the timetable.

John Baliol's Elevated Station

A plaque reads : ' This station stands on the Great Hall of Berwick Castle. Here on November 17th. 1292 the claim of Robert the Bruce of Scotland was declined and the decision in favour of John Baliol was given by Edward I before the full Parliament of England and Scotland and a large gathering of the nobility and populace of both England and Scotland.'

Part of the curtain wall of this famous fortress can still be seen on the other side of the railway line.

One of Northumbria's greatest historians, Robert Hugill, noted the destruction of the castle like this :

' Almost a hundred years ago (he wrote in 1939) the last of the ancient structures that had withstood siege and counter-siege, had been occupied in turn by the Scots and English, was razed to make room for a railway station.'

Murder In The Great Hall

In 1377 Edward III's governor in Berwick was Sir Robert Boynton.

Sir Robert was unpopular in Berwick. It is said that he exercised the droit de seigneur to the extent of raping a bride on her wedding day. It is claimed that he taxed the populace unfairly and kept back part of the money for himself. There are even suggestions that he ordered the deaths of a number of people who spoke out against him.

Such a poor press seems conclusive enough, but it is probably far from the truth. Sir Robert was English, and that was enough cause to defame him. He was also very much Edward III's man, a fact that would have endeared him to few borderers.

Alternative accounts, which may be equally laced with propaganda, paint a very different picture. Here we see Sir Robert the family man, loyal to his king, but fair - even generous - to the people of Berwick. No doubt he also gave flowers to his aged mother, presented the prizes at sports days, and held fund raising events for widows and orphans.

One of the lessons of history is that many accounts should be treated with suspicion. Much of what is written has a political focus or interpretation. The vilification of Richard III by the Tudors is typical of the inaccuracy of a received historical tradition.

But we can be sure of one thing. The Governor of Berwick died in particularly brutal circumstances. Seven assassins climbed the castle walls at night. They crept up on the guards and cut their throats.

After searching several of the main apartments they found Sir Robert in the Great Hall. He had just completed his meal of venison and wine.

They accused him of ordering the murder of a local farmer. He denied it.

They struck him to the ground with the flat blades of their heavy swords. He begged for mercy. The claymores were lifted over him and as the blows rained down as he called to his Maker to receive his soul. The brutality of the killing was such that they were not satisfied until the corpse was mutilated beyond recognition.

Rebellion And Retaliation

This was the spark of revolution. The news of Sir Robert's murder spread like fire itself and the men of Berwick soon captured the castle for themselves. Many of the garrison were butchered. Heads and limbs were placed on spikes and displayed on the battlements.

Edward III's response was predictable. He ordered a force of 7000 archers and 3000 cavalry to Berwick. The siege lasted for eight days before the English force managed to break through the main gate.

What followed was a second massacre. Those of the castle garrison of 50 who had survived the siege were hung or hacked to death. The reprisals continued into the town. Houses were burnt. Men and women were held and tortured until they betrayed those who had opposed Sir Robert. Then there were more hangings.

The Witch Hysteria

The castle is also linked with witchcraft.

In 1586 Sir John Forster* had two men and a woman - 'all lewd persons' - committed to prison on suspicion of having caused a death by witchcraft.

In 1590 the wife of Richard Swynbourne was found ' by the oath of credible witnesses to have dealings with several women witches in order to bewitch one of the garrison men at Berwick.'

In the same year James VI asked 'for a woman witch of Scotland, either in prison or otherwise at Berwick, to be delivered to His Majesty's Justice.'

This was the time of witch hysteria. James VI of Scotland, later to become also James I of England, was an over-zealous witch hunter. At a time when thinking had developed far beyond the superstitions of the Middle Ages, King James did his best to set the clock back.

Modern thinking points to a strange psychological makeup that caused the king to be fascinated by all things vile and perverse. The trauma of his early life, with murdered father and imprisoned mother, may point to some sort of explanation. The bisexual monarch personally set the tone for one of the most licentious courts in history. His favourite, George Villiers, was also his procurer and a massive influence on James's thinking. The king persecuted 'catholics' as vigorously as witches. This in turn lead to the Gunpowder Plot.

King James also commissioned the Authorised Version of the Bible, a work that has never been surpassed for the near perfection and musicality of its language.

It is not surprising that he is remembered as 'The Wisest Fool in Christendom.'

It is against these staggering contradictions of behaviour that the witch hysteria should be judged.

The Witches

There are many conflicting reports. Here is a shortlist of the three most famous cases.

Eliza, the Auchencrow Witch, was said to have influence that carried as far as Ayton, Eyemouth, and Berwick. Her 'crimes' included causing cot deaths, sheep abortions, and the disappearance of children.

She was killed at Blackadder following a conflict between covens. A rival 'witch' stabbed her in the belly with a pitchfork.

Black Sarah of Spittal was accused of making potions that made men adulterous. She was taken to Berwick Castle for questioning and died after a guard dog became unleashed and savaged her.

Tom Ward, known as Ward the Warlock, was driven out of the Berwick because it was said that he curdled the milk and soured the ale. It is not known what became of him.

Down By The Riverside

By the post box opposite the station there are downhill steps that lead to formal gardens. Pass the empty boating pool and descend again. An iron railing on the right points towards access to the riverside.

Turn right. This is one of the finest stretches of riverside walking in Northumbria. The Tweed can be seen to its very best advantage right here.

There is a fragment of the castle below the railway bridge with the wall climbing away from the river towards the main keep at the station above.

This is known as the White Wall. The steps nearby are appropriately called Breakneck Stairs. A huge boom once stretched from the riverside water tower to the opposite bank. This could be put in place to prevent enemy ships sailing further upstream.

A Public Spectacle

The unfortunate Countess Buchan was found guilty by Edward I of the crime of crowning Robert the Bruce. Her punishment was to die of hunger, thirst and exposure. An iron cage was constructed so small that the victim barely had room to flex her limbs.

She was exposed on the castle walls. The crowds increased each day. Bets were taken on how long she would last. She was pronounced dead after 11 days.

The body was left in the cage to rot for the next four years. It became a popular feature of the regional sight-seeing itinerary - a kind of early tourist board initiative.

Two Follies

Walk south west towards the Royal Tweed Bridge. Its design seems to prove that architecture can too easily become the art of wasting space.

This monstrosity was opened in 1928. Its intrinsic ugliness is exaggerated because it stands directly between the elegant lines of Stephenson's Royal Border Railway Bridge, and the trim 15 arches of the early 17th. century Berwick Bridge. When it comes to design that is both functional and aesthetically pleasing it seems best to ignore the 20th. century.

A more modern folly is represented by the words 'G Thompson is OK ' written high on an exposed rock on the left. Conquerer's Well, also on the left, is a memorial to the 19th. century clock and watch maker, Peter Conquerer.

Turn up beyond the boathouse to Meg's Mount. From the summit there are fine views over the bridges towards Tweedmouth.

Edward's Ultimatum

Edward III proved he could not be outdone by his grandfather in the barbarity stakes.

After blockading the town for more than three months he became impatient. He held two sons of Berwick's deputy governor, Sir Alexander Seton, and made his ultimatum. Unless the keys of the town were promptly handed over, he would hang the boys within sight of the walls.

Seton's wife begged him to give in. But the governor, aware of the terrible privations already suffered by the townsfolk, was not prepared to let the town fall to blackmail.

Edward III kept his word. Seton's sons were hung at Tweedmouth. The site of the gallows is still called Hangie Dyke Neuk.

Murder At The Netty

The most surprising thing about the vampire cult is that it continues to grow in inverse proportion to the evidence.

Bram Stoker's Dracula remains the focus of the cult. When the writer had the coffin of the undead Transylvanian count dropped off at Whitby he unwittingly began a process of rewriting history.

Bloodthirsty incidents from the past are now regularly rewritten to give them a vampire flavour. One problem with this is that it sometimes makes it more difficult to make sense of what really happened.

Take the case of Betty Hough.

Betty was a local lady whose only known interest was sex. As this was also her main source of income, the fact that she enjoyed it was no bad thing.

Life was sweet for Betty until she became involved with a likely lad called Colin McFaddon. He was a small time farmer who supplemented his modest income by poaching and pimping.

At weekends the two of them would meet at a Tweedmouth hostelry - probably the Royal - which is now an old peoples' home.

On the fateful evening, Betty Hough excused herself and went outside to the primitive netty. Some time later McFaddon followed her. Minutes later he re-entered the bar to complain that the netty door was bolted.

A number of men watched as the landlord broke down the door with his shoulder. Betty was found inside. Her throat had been severed and the head pushed savagely back. Blood was everywhere. There were even fresh stains on the wooden walls.

The horror of the incident provoked an outcry. Modern accounts talk of a vampire on the loose. The evidence is largely based on a number of lambs that had been found with their throats torn out.

But nobody cried wolf when a rapist was arrested three months later. This man was immediately acclaimed as the murderer of Betty Hough. It is said he had enlarged canine teeth and had threatened to bite the neck of his young victim if she fought against his will.

The final drama was played out when the man escaped his guards after biting one of them. Colin McFaddon was amongst the men who began the search. The rapist was found in a shallow pit in nearby woods. He was half buried in the earth. This 'undead' creature then rose up to face the men who had found him.

It is said that McFaddon lead the murderous attack on the rapist. They struck him again and again with their spades and pitchforks. It was an almost unrecognisable body that was later burned on a bonfire.

But who did kill Betty Hough?

Setting the vampire story aside, the most likely murderer is McFaddon himself. It is known that he argued publicly with the victim about money, and that he'd refused to marry her.

Might he not have followed her out of the pub and begun his savage attack as she left the netty? Possibly he pushed her back inside the primitive cubicle, cut her throat, and secured the bolt inside before climbing out at the top.

The force with which the head was jerked back had broken the neck. In effect Betty Hough had been murdered twice.

Unnatural savagery would account for this, but so would an attempt to mask the crime. Whoever killed her may just have wanted to make it look more than a simple crime of passion.

But what of the blood on the walls? Modern versions of the story suggest this came from the vampire over gorging himself and spitting out the last few mouthfuls. A more likely explanation is that it came from the killer's hands or clothing as he climbed.

There was a pump in the yard that could have been used for removing the traces of blood.

It is also possible that Betty was killed by one of her customers. The weekend was prime time for business. As business was also pleasure, Betty may have been delighted to make the most of a brief interlude in the evening's drinking.

But again the finger points at McFaddon. He had a jealous and violent, nature. If Betty Hough had gone outside with another man, a drunken rage would at least provide a believable explanation of the crime.

And the rapist? According to modern versions this man was an outsider, possibly a tramp or a tinker. Contemporary accounts however are more specific. He was called Archibald Haydon. He is listed in records as a pauper of the parish.

It is likely his habits were known as much as his identity. Certainly it did not take McFaddon's posse long to track him to his lair.

The shallow grave and part covered body are almost certainly further modern elaborations. It is more likely that Haydon dug some sort of pit to help conceal himself in the woods. Most accounts agree that it was his foot sticking out of the undergrowth that gave him away.

If McFaddon was the murderer of Betty Hough there is little doubt that he would have been keen to divert suspicion elsewhere. His determination to lead the search for the killer would be typical. His equal determination to make sure that the man answered no more questions is also predictable behaviour.

And the vampire teeth? This was not an uncommon feature of the age. Receding gums and the common loss of front teeth often meant the canines were exaggerated. It meant nothing at the time, but that was before the gothic tradition begun by Bram Stoker's bloodsucking count.

𝔗he 𝔉ortifications

Follow the path to the ramparts and cross Marygate. There are excellent views down the length of Berwick's main shopping street to the town hall.

One of the fascinations of Berwick is the way that the fortifications reflect the change in the fashion of warfare over many centuries.

High walls and towers were popular in the middle ages. In Berwick these are represented at least in spirit by the fragments of the castle. By the 16th. century this arrangement had proved itself vulnerable to artillery bombardment. Lower profile walls on artificial mounds were a partial answer to this problem. The earliest that can be clearly identified at Berwick is the detached earthwork of the Windmill Bulwark.

The Fortifications, Berwick

Towards the middle of the 16th. century the idea of the bastion was imported from Italy. These were essentially earthworks protected by a ditch. Heavy cannon placed on a rampart at the top of the steep bastion slope had a wide range of fire.

Little of the early bastion earthwork remains, but the various phases of the military development since that time are the central theme of the Berwick fortifications.

Elizabeth I, who good reason to secure her northern border, ordered military engineer Sir Robert Lee to Berwick. After many changes and revisions to plans, the work was carried out.

The idea was to have semi-concealed double story emplacements within the earthwork itself, with main and flanking cannon at the top protected by a parapet wall. Passages within the earthworks connected the bastions with the inner ring of the town's fortifications.

The threat from the north subsided after the imprisonment of Mary, Queen of Scots in 1568. The work was stopped whilst still hopelessly incomplete. For defence purposes Berwick had once again to relay mainly on its crumbling medieval walls.

There were three final stages in the development of the defences. The Elizabethan design was given some practical modifications during the 17th. century Commonwealth. The Ravensdowne Barracks were built after the 1715 Jacobite incursions. Following the second Jacobite challenge to the English crown in 1745 there were substantial repairs and improvements to the earthworks.

But what the visitor sees today is essentially the Elizabethan ramparts. In terms of national expenditure this is the single most expensive defence project of the first Elizabethan era. Only the purchase of Trident in the age of the second Elizabeth compares with it in terms of the nation's investment in just one cog in the defence machine.

Returning To Old Haunts

The lone figure of a young soldier of Cromwell's army has often been seen walking in the area of Cumberland Bastion.

There are no satisfactory explanations of the haunting. But perhaps the ghost provides his own clue.

When the phantom foot-soldier is approached, he draws a knife from his belt and raises the blade point to beneath his chin. Twice he calls out the name ' Mary ' clearly. As he repeats it a third time the last syllable turns into a throaty moan as the blade is pulled downwards to sever the jugular. As he falls, he begins to fade into the ether. Patches of fresh blood have been found at the place where he vanishes.

The Church without a Tower

William Wallace - A Man Of Many Parts

Turn down right to the former Urban Sanitary Authority Building, now the council offices. This is Wallace Green.

William Wallace played a key role in the guerilla resistance to Edward I in the borders. One of his triumphs was to seize Berwick in 1297. He was betrayed to the English in August 1305, and taken to London. Following a brief trial he was brutally executed.

His quartered left arm was brought to Berwick to be exhibited.

You pass St. Andrew's (Church of Scotland) on the way to the Parish Church of the Holy Trinity and St. Mary.

Oliver's Influence

The foundation stone of the present church was laid in 1650. The building has an unusual appearance because of the lack of towers. The story is that when Cromwell passed through Berwick - on his way to do battle at Dunbar - he made it clear that he approved neither of towers or church bells.

An earlier church, completed early in the 13th. century, stood slightly to the south of the present building.

The Canon's Tale

The plague struck Berwick twice at the end of the 12th. century. The source of the disease was not understood. It was generally thought to be divine punishment.

This thinking lead to some bizarre incidents. One story comes from a contemporary account penned by Canon William of Newburgh.**

One victim of the plague was a wealthy merchant. Although he had seemingly lead an upright life there were those after his death who claimed he had been in league with Satan.

His body was taken from the consecrated ground and buried elsewhere. Each night he was said to rise from the grave for a feast of human flesh.

Ten young men were selected to put an end to the merchant's nocturnal activities. They dug up the corpse, cut it into pieces, heaped the remains on a bonfire, and later cast the ashes into the sea. This proved effective in removing human flesh from the local menu.

But the procedure had a second purpose. It was hoped that the curse of the plague, inflicted perhaps because of the merchant's evil doings, would be lifted. For a while this seemed to be the case, but the scourge returned the following year.

The King's Own Borderers

Turn left past the barracks. The King's Own Borderer's Museum is well worth a visit. It is much more than the usual regimental museum. The exhibits have been well thought out and are effectively displayed. It is the best museum in the borders for capturing the mood of an era.

Life in the barracks was very tough. The following short insights from contemporary documents may help to capture the essence of it:

'there were 24 rooms for officers, and 72 for private soldiers. The latter contain 576 men...'

'in the main guard house there is an apartment called the Black Hole...'

'the punishment of flagellation is only inflicted in the square...'

'having been taken at Morpeth, and returned to the barracks, could say nothing in mitigation of deserting and is thus condemned to a dishonourable end...'

'lost a month's pay on the turn of a card...'

'and continues to disobey that order and consorts with loose women...'

'take boiled mutton, horseflesh, and a mix of turnip and potatoes...'

'so grossly afflicted with dysentery I doubt we could muster for engagement...'

'and again gave the order that the barrels be cleaned...'

'here we breed impatience and flies...'

Suspicious Death At The Windmill

Such a regime was bound to create the occasional violent response. The body of a sergeant armourer was found close to the Windmill bastion in 1727. The man had a bullet lodged in his brain.

The official report records the death as suicide, but it is known that the sergeant had been one corner of a triangle of passion.

The woman involved was Lizzie Grey - ' as bountiful as she was buxom.'

Lizzie was no ordinary camp follower. She had a code of fidelity that restricted her to one man only - for the duration of his stay in the barracks. When her man left, she felt free to find a replacement.

The arrangement seemed to work well for many years, until either through ill luck or mismanagement Lizzie found herself obliged to two men at the same time.

The remedy she suggested was a rota system, but this broke down when the sergeant armourer let himself into her lodgings to find she was entertaining a young officer. The officer pulled rank, but the sergeant pulled a knife and threatened to perform a surgical procedure on the officer. An unpleasant incident was avoided when Lizzie pulled her voluptuous bulk out of bed and placed it between the two men.

A week later the sergeant was found dead. No serious questions were asked of the young officer, who was of course a gentleman and therefore utterly decent and honourable.

But the sniff of rumour wafted round the barracks faster than the rancid turnip stew. A month later the young man resigned his commission and returned to his father's estate near Jedburgh.

He married, fathered four children in five years, and rapidly earned a reputation as a man of commerce. In order to make sure he retained a competitive edge he regularly made personal visits to valued clients - in Berwick.

He would always stay at a particular inn - one of the town's best. The same hostelry had been purchased in 1728 by Lizzie Grey.

She told everyone she had been fortunate in receiving a large bequest from an uncle that she had not seen for many years.

Net Hooks?

Rejoin the rampart walls at the Windmill Bastion and walk towards the river. From King's Bastion there are fine views over the estuary and Tweedmouth. The Elizabethan walls end here at King's Mount. Just below is the Black Watch Tower, the only remaining example of a bastion dating from the brief reign of King Edward VI.

The cottages below feature what appear to be metal hooks on the roofs. The locals like to tease visitors by saying these are for hanging nets. But you will wait

Walking The Walls

forever to catch a glimpse of a single swarthy seafarer climbing to the roof tops with his net. The 'hooks' are overflow pipes for attic header tanks.

Smugglers' Delight

Pass the old school buildings with their separate entrances for boys and girls. After the Custom House you pass along the ancient Quay Walls. A number of passages lead through the walls to the quay from the cellars and yards of the houses behind.

Despite the proximity of the Custom House these passages have a long association with the landing of 'duty free' and dodgy goods. Of course nothing like that ever happens today...

Wails On The Walls

Berwick has many famous ghosts but there are none to rival the Wailing Boy.

His appearances have been most frequently noted on crisp winter evenings just after sunset. The boy, whose favourite haunt is the Quay Walls area, is invariably seen looking over the wall to the river.

In November 1756 a fishing coble was lost without trace. There were three men on board - a father and his two eldest sons. A younger son had come down to the walls to watch the catches being unloaded.

As darkness fell he had a premonition that something terrible had happened. Tears filled his eyes and he began to sob. Passers-by tried to comfort him but this only made matters worse. The sobs turned to a pitiful wailing and his whole young body began to shake.

Finally, the wife of a local magistrate coaxed him away from the wall and took him home. When his mother heard the knock on the door she thought it was the menfolk returned from their day's fishing.

She took one look at her sorrowful son and burst into tears. The magistrate's wife was so affected by this lachrymose duet that she too joined in the lamentation.

Many of the women in the street rushed from their homes to add their voices to the cacophony of caterwauling. Nothing had been said about the ill fated coble, and at this stage there should have been little cause for concern.

Since that time the appearance of the Wailing Boy has always been greeted with a sense of foreboding.

He has appeared before news of many a loss at sea. He appeared just before the first great battle of World War 1. Many local families suffered their first

Wailing Walls

loses at Mons. He was seen on November 22nd. 1963 - just a few hours before the assassination of President Kennedy.

During the 19th. century the phenomenon won the attention of a number of celebrities. These included the playwright Thomas Robertson, and Thomas Macaulay the historian and statesman. Ehrich Weiss, who is better remembered as Harry Houdini, studied the 'case' in some detail.

In a hastily withdrawn Victorian pamphlet the noise made by the Wailing Boy was described as a 'strange nocturnal emission'. It is also believed that the world's worst poet, William McGonagall, wrote a poem about it. Sadly it does not appear in any of the published collections.

Taking Stock

Turn right at the Berwick Bridge, then straight up West Street and turn right again for the Town Hall.

This distinctive building was begun in 1750. The stocks are authentic, although moved from another location. It is possible to visit the dungeons.

Marygate can be lively, especially on market days. A walk to the top of the street returns you to the starting point of the trail

* See Ghost Trails of Northumbria. **

See More Ghost Trails of Northumbria.

No. 5
Newcastle-Upon-Tyne

This circular walking tour takes about three hours

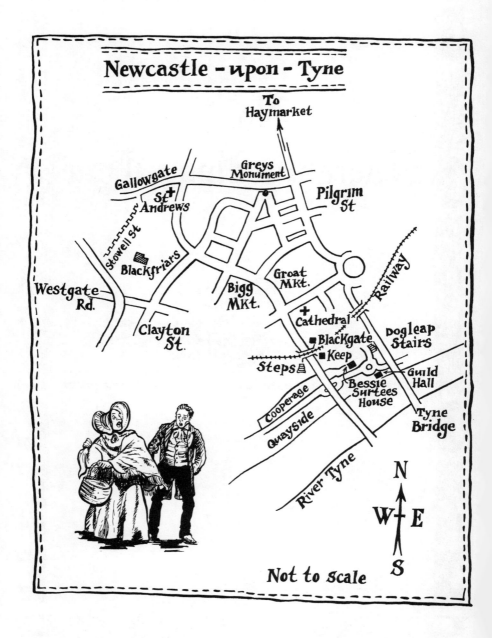

Newcastle - upon - Tyne

To Haymarket

Greys Monument

Gallowgate

St Andrews

Pilgrim St

Stowell St

Blackfriars

Westgate Rd.

Groat Mkt.

Bigg Mkt.

Railway

Clayton St.

Cathedral

Blackgate

Dogleap Stairs

Keep

Steps

Guild Hall

Cooperage

Bessie Surtees House

Quayside

Tyne Bridge

River Tyne

N
W E
S

Not to scale

The Region's Capital

Newcastle-upon-Tyne is the region's capital. For some reason it does not capture the tourist imagination like say York or Lincoln, but it has more to offer than either.

Anyway you look at it Newcastle is a special place. It is a busy cosmopolitan city, yet it is also compact and accessible. It has a style and character of its own, with buildings that rival any in the country for their grandeur.

Because of its regional importance Newcastle has a range of shops, entertainments, cultural and sports facilities that put it in the premier league of the nation's cities.

A Brief History

Before the work on Hadrian's Wall began, the Romans had already bridged the Tyne and built a fort here.

After the Romans left Britain it fell into dark age obscurity, emerging in later Saxon times as Monkcaster, a name which reflects the number of monastic foundations based here.

It was the Normans who realised its full strategic importance. The Conqueror's son, Robert, built a wooden fort here. From that time the name Newcastle was born.

William Rufus ordered the construction of the first stone castle. During the anarchic reign of Stephen it fell to Scotland but reverted to the English crown after the capture of William the Lion at Alnwick.**

Despite the new walls there were further Scots incursions and the legendary Harry Hotspur led the defence before the Battle of Otterburn.**

During the English Civil Wars it became a royalist stronghold. A force of 2000 held out against a siege for three months before the walls were finally breached.

The days of greatest glory were during the Industrial Revolution. The Stephenson Brothers, Lord Armstrong, and many others led the world in technological innovation. Shipbuilding and engineering excellence became the hallmark of a rapidly growing city. The University, theatres, and many of the lofty commercial buildings date from this period.

There were mixed feelings about the reconstruction work of the 1970's and 80's. A large new shopping centre at Eldon Square, was followed by an even more ambitious project nearby at Gateshead - the Metro Centre.

The Metro railway system and the Queen Elizabeth II Bridge scheme cut congestion and created a totally new image. The rapid development of the airport, the wheeling and dealing of entrepreneur Sir John Hall, and the second coming of 'Saint' Kevin Keegan to the famous football club, were all important factors in putting the city back on the international map.

Newcastle today is an unusual cocktail mix of old and new. This final trail explores some of the best of both.

The Body In The Bank

Begin at Grey's Monument. This distinctive 40 metre tower was built as a tribute to the Prime Minister who introduced the Reform Bill of 1832. Today it often serves as a meeting place and is popular with local buskers.

Walk down Pilgrim Street. Pass the Police and Fire Stations and Swan House. Blue Posts Yard (no. 140 - 144) is part of a Victorian Building. It features a white stone fascia and

Grey's Monument

there is a gilded plumed crest over the main door.

The infamous Body in the Bank murder took place here and the inquest was held at Blue Posts Yard.

The first sign that there was anything wrong was when fire was seen pouring out of a window early in the morning of 7th. October 1838.

The fire brigade reacted quickly and within minutes firemen had forced their way into the room.

It was still dark so lanterns had to be lit. The sight that was illuminated was not a pretty one.

There were two men slumped on the floor near the table. One of them was groaning and showing signs of coming to. The other was very obviously dead. The furniture and carpet were splattered with blood and brains. Later it was shown that there were more than 20 blows to the dead man's skull. A heavy poker lying nearby proved to be the weapon of murder.

The dead man's pockets contained partly charred paper. It was obvious an attempt had been made had been made to burn the body.

The survivor was a bank official called Archibald Bolam. The dead man had been his assistant Joseph Millie.

Bolam was examined by two doctors but was found to be suffering from little more than the effect of fumes. There was a slight scratch wound on his neck.

Bolam's story was a confused one. He claimed that threatening letters had been pushed under his door on the day of the murder. He had left the bank to warn his housekeeper, Mary Walker, to be extra cautious.

When he returned to the bank he found his dead assistant. As he turned to go for help he was attacked by a man who had followed him into the room. The man was said to have a blackened face.

After a fierce struggle Bolam had passed out and knew nothing more until after the firemen had arrived.

The authorities were not satisfied with the story. Bolam was arrested and brought to trial for murder. The prosecution pointed to inconsistencies in his story and the account first given by his housekeeper. It also became clear that Bolam was not the respectable citizen he claimed to be. He used the services of prostitutes, drank heavily, had gambling debts, and had made his housekeeper his mistress.

But it was all circumstantial. The bank admitted nothing about financial irregularities and witnesses stressed that Bolam had been on the best of terms with his assistant. In his summing up Judge Maule instructed the jury that the evidence for a murder conviction was unsatisfactory. Bolam, however, was found guilty of manslaughter and sentenced to transportation.

A Case Of Blackmail

There are still arguments about the case. Bolam always maintained that the story of the threatening letters and unknown assailant was true. He died 24 years later in Australia. The epitaph on his gravestone in a Sydney churchyard finishes with the words :

' Here lies an Honest Man.'

But it is likely that the police were right to believe Bolam committed murder. The idea that he attacked Millie in a fit of mindless and motiveless frenzy - the essence of the manslaughter verdict - does not fit the Bolam profile.

There is a strong possibility that the bank denied irregularities to protect its reputation. Millie had been Bolam's protege. They had been friends. But Millie may have been asked to compromise his position, or he may just have stumbled upon some damning evidence against Bolam.

Other clues point in different directions. Bolam's former assistant, George Ridley, had lost his job several months earlier. It is known that Bolam plotted his downfall and eventual replacement by Millie. Ridley hated Bolam and enjoyed his downfall. Could he have been implicated?

There is a suggestion too that Bolam's sexual repertoire included relationships with young men. Millie at 56 - 15 years Bolam's senior - hardly qualified, but might he have developed a sudden surge of ambition? After years of struggling in the bank's lower echelons he had just been appointed as Bolam's assistant - a position of some influence. He was close enough to Bolam to know a great deal about him, and clever enough to know how to best take advantage of this knowledge.

It could just be that Millie misjudged Bolam's response to blackmail and inadvertently provoked the terrible attack on himself.

Fire Over The Tyne

Turn down to the Tyne Bridge Lift. There are splendid views over the river to Gateshead.

A fire started at a woollen factory in Gateshead on October 6th. 1854 that was to become Tyneside's greatest natural disaster.

The fire spread to a nearby building called Bertram's Warehouse, which stored a lethal chemical cocktail of nitrates, sulphates and oil. Once this was alight the spread could not be halted.

For those on the Newcastle side of the river it was at first a sightseeing spectacle. Thousands thronged around the quayside to watch the display as huge

The Tyne Bridge Lift

explosions sent blue fireballs high into the air. A deafening roar preceded the leap of one massive fireball that was seen more than 60 miles away.

But the mood changed to panic as the tempermature rose. Then searing hot material began to rain down across the river and fires broke out in pockets around the city centre.

Then the lights went out.

People were crushed in the rush away from the flames. Others perished on the river itself and in the timer frame buildings and warehouses close to the banks of the Tyne.

Much of the quayside disappeared in the flames.

Fire services from the region were joined by those from as far away as southern Scotland and Lancashire. Even with their combined efforts it took more than 24 hours to bring the fire under control. Firefighters admitted that rain and the changing direction of the wind had greatly aided their cause.

The official death toll was 53 - with most fatalities on the Gateshead side. This figure does not include a number of people staying at the Hillside charity lodging house that simply disappeared after an explosion. It is believed that a number of vagrants, dossing down in warehouses close to the source of the fire, were incinerated. The real death toll was probably more than 100.

The Great Flood

The Tyne Bridge, Newcastle's vital trading and communication route to the south, survived a great flood in 1339.

The Modern Tyne Bridge

During the following centuries a constant process of repair and rebuilding made the bridge into an important trading centre. Ramshackle timber framed buildings clung precariously to the parapets.

Following heavy rain in November 1771 the river rose more than six feet in a few hours. Water soaked through the wooden floors adding more weight and instability to an already over-strained structure.

The river was becoming a sea. Some realised the danger in time. Collecting what few possessions they could, they fought their way to the fast receding shore line. Some who woke later managed to escape by taking a grip on the walls and wading through the fast flowing water. Those who lost their grip or footing were swept away. The fact that there were only six casualties is an indication of a number of near miraculous escapes.

When the central arch of the bridge collapsed, buildings subsided into the waters below. Most had already escaped, but a pile of floating debris later indicated that members of one family died in their beds.

The bridge that had survived for four centuries was beyond repair.

A Gruesome Display

One tradition of the old bridge was also washed away with the flood. It had been the favoured site for the display of the limbs of those executed for their 'crimes'.

In the early years it had often featured the famous. This grisly catalogue includes the right arms of William Wallace and the Earl of Wiltshire, the legs of an early Lord Grey, and the full set of limbs of Andrew de Harcla and the 4th. Earl Percy.

The displays were intended to discourage rebellion.

The Guild Hall

The Branks Of The Tyne

Retrace your steps to the Guild Hall. This famous building was formerly Newcastle's courthouse.

At the time of the first Queen Elizabeth a special piece of equipment was kept here. It was the famous branks - a heavy iron muzzle used to quieten the tongue of nagging wives. To the constant regret of many a Geordie husband the branks was withdrawn early in 16th. century, but at least the menfolk could comfort themselves with the thought of the nearby ducking pool.

The infamous Judge Jeffries came here in 1684 but left without ordering a single hanging.

Kincaid the witchfinder held his own special 'court' here in 1649.* Again it was not a good day for convictions. The witchfinder was paid a pound for each conviction which no doubt encouraged him to be particularly diligent.**

On this occasion Kincaid was discouraged by the intervention of Deputy Governor Hobson. He was unhappy with the way Kincaid handled the pricking tool. After one poor woman was convicted Hobson snatched the weapon from Kincaid and applied it himself

The method was to the strip the woman and to look for 'Satan's mark' - normally a mole or other blemish on the skin. The pricking tool was then stabbed into the flesh. If the woman did not react with a scream and no blood was drawn she was pronounced guilty. *

When the Deputy Governor took the tool from Kincaid he was questioning the verdict. When he applied the point to the mark that the witchfinder had found he was rewarded with a shout of pain and a flow of blood. For many of those who escaped it was little more than a reprieve. In the following year there was another rounding up of witches. The 15 convicted were hung together at the Town Moor.

A Whip Round

The Sandhill was also the favoured place for a whipping. This was a punishment applied to men for immoral behaviour or begging. Women were usually tarred and feathered

Whippings were almost as popular as hangings with the crowd giving enthusiastic vocal support to the man who wielded the lash.

Pickpockets took full advantage of these occasions. In July 1673 an impoverished minister had his pockets emptied as he prayed for the victim of the lash. The crowd felt sorry for him and gave him money from their own pockets.

It is said that he left the Sandhill ' weighed down with coin as never before.'

Axing Lyrical

A de-luxe scaffold was erected for an execution in May 1464.

A huge crowd gathered for the event. Money changed hands for a grandstand view from the Sandhill balconies. Hangings were common enough, but the prospect of watching the headsman's special skill was irresistible.

The event marked the revenge of the Percy family on three noblemen who had deserted their cause before the Battle of Hedgeley Moor.* Lords Hungerford, Roos, and Taillebois had the honour of facing the axe rather than the rope because of their elevated status.

A ballad was hastily composed in celebration of the occasion. A modern version of the ballad which runs to a traditional dance tune of the time begins:

> 'Oh happy headsman swing your axe
> For Hungerford and Roos
> May Taillebois thank the Maker
> For he has slipped the noose.'

Death Of A Joker

A very public murder took place on Sandgate in 1764.

Robert Lindsay was well known as a prankster. His sense of humour included urinating in beer barrels and cutting holes in clothing left to dry on the line.

Early one July morning, a pawnbroker's wife, Mrs Stewart, woke to find Lindsay at her bedroom window. He was sitting high on a wall singing a bawdy song.

She told him to be gone. When he refused she threatened him with a pair of hot fire tongs. Lindsay laughed in her face.

Meanwhile the pawnbroker had gone for his blunderbuss. When he returned he brushed his wife out of the way and threatened to shoot Lindsay off the wall. The angry voices had begun to wake some of the neighbours. A small group were already gathered below when Stewart repeated his threat. The pawnbroker tried to fire a warning shot but the powder fizzled without firing the charge.

By now Lindsay was doubled up with laughter.

Stewart was overcome with rage. He ordered his wife to help him recharge the weapon.

There were now around 20 people watching from the street. Stewart barked a final threat before aiming the gun. Lindsay gave him a two fingered salute.

A moment later the prankster lay dead on the stones below.

Murder was the coroner's verdict, and guilty was the judgement of the assize jury.

Stewart made his final appearance in front of an crowd estimated to be 100 times greater than the number who watched the shooting. As he felt the noose tighten around his neck on that fine August morning it may not have been much consolation.

Another Face At The Window

Bessie Surtees' House, now in the care of English Heritage, is opposite the Guild Hall. It was from a high window in this building that Bessie climbed down to elope with John Scott.

Bessie Surtee's House

Bessie was one of the beauties of her age. Her father was a banking entrepreneur who was determined that his daughter would consolidate his fortune on her marriage.

John Scott was living at a more humble address when he met Bessie. It was a storybook romance that looked like ending when Bessie's father forbade any further meetings.

That hatched the plot of the elopement. At 11 o'clock on a quiet evening Scott brought his horse to below the window. Bessie threw down one small bag then climbed down to mount the horse behind him.

The noise must have raised the alarm. The young lovers were immediately pursued along the quayside by men and a pack of dogs. Scott took a gamble. He turned the horse's head to the right and began to ride up one of the steepest stairways in Newcastle.

The horse remained sure in his footing, and as they emerged at the top of the stairs they were well ahead of the chasing pack.

They married in Scotland and in time both sets of parents accepted the marriage. Perhaps this had something to do with Scott's

The Cooperage

meteoric career. He was a man of some ability who was soon noticed by those in positions of power and influence.

John Scott eventually attained such a position himself. He became Lord Eldon, and Lord Chancellor of England. The ghost of Bessie Surtees is still said to haunt the Sandgate. The most common phenomenon is the vision of her face in a window of the old house. The window is now distinctively marked with a pane of blue glass.

The Cooperage is just a short distance along the Sandgate. It is a half timbered traditional English hostelry, and as one of Newcastle's finest and oldest buildings it has attracted a fair following of phantoms. Ghostly ladies in long silk dresses are often seen on the alleyway stairs.

There is an ancient wooden door on the stairs at the side of the building with no handle or lock on the outside. This does not seem to deter the 'silkies' who apparently drift through it. This phenomenon is most frequently noted after closing time.

Back In Time

As you climb the stairs the relics of earlier generations of street lighting are worth noting. Before the top flight turn right under the High Level Bridge, then straight on through the ruins to a black and gold railing. This is the top of Dog Leap stairs up which Bessie Surtees and John Scott made their famous escape.

Carry on up through the outer wall archway and up again to the castle keep.

Up The Stairs

The keep was massively built with walls up to five and a half metres thick at the base. The Great Hall is above and the famous castle dungeons below.

Roger Rambo

During the Civil Wars, Roger Wetherley and 11 others loyal to the king hid in the Sallyport Tower. The situation seemed hopeless since the city had fallen to the Roundheads. It was only a matter of time before they were taken as prisoners.

Wetherley was a marked man. As the Roundheads invaded the city he had led 30 men against an enemy force more than three times as numerous. Such was the ferocity of the attack the Roundheads retreated after suffering many casualties.

There were similar heroics when Wetherley and his 11 companions came out from the Sallyport Tower. They stole horses and began to ride to the west of the city.

It was there that they ran into a Roundhead patrol.

Wetherley asked for his men to pass to avoid further killing. The Roundhead captain, confident of his force of 30, refused. The Roundheads charged but Wetherley's men fought their way through the line. The five who survived the skirmish were instructed by Wetherley to escape. He waited to face the Roundheads alone.

In all the swash and buckle that followed Wetherley cut down all who attacked him. Even when he was knocked from his horse he fought on defiantly. Finally he stood at the centre of a bloody ring of corpses and challenged the Roundhead captain to finish it.

The captain, who had been wounded in the first skirmish, declined. Wetherley took a horse and rode away in pursuit of his men.

The Quay To The Hauntings

The ghost of Roger Wetherley is one of dozens said to haunt the Quayside, particularly around the old hostelries.

The area is so congested with phantoms you imagine it must take some organisation. Some years ago something of the kind was suggested by a student rag committee. The idea was to conjure up the shade of Roger Wetherley and to ask him to supervise the hauntings in a coordinated way.

They stayed overnight in the Cooperage, but the cavalier did not materialise for the planned discussion. It's a pity, because they had dreamed up a fine title for him - Roger Wetherley, the Phantom Inn Spectre.

A Sad Fate At The Gate

Keep to the right and pass through the green arch of the Railway Bridge. The Black Gate is on the right. Under this arch you can see the recess that held the portcullis. Early in the 14th. century the rope securing the portcullis gave way. The Sheriff of Northumberland's envoy who was standing underneath it at the time was almost perfectly dissected into equal portions.

Life And Death In Prison

The gate was built in 1242, and many prisoners passed this way on their way to the dark dungeons.

Conditions must have been appalling. With 20 or more men and women to a poorly ventilated cell, the stench was said to be dreadful. Criminals of all kinds were herded together. It was a battle of the fittest for survival.

There were hundreds of murders, rape was a matter of routine, and fights would break out regularly over a scrap of stale bread.

But by the late 18th. century things had begun to improve. Prison reformer, John Howard, wrote :

' They are kept in dirty, damp dungeons, having no roof in the wet season, and sit in up to six inches of water. The felons are chained to iron rings hammered into each wall.'

A century earlier conditions had been worse. Nathaniel Hareshaw, wrote in his diocesan report : ' The pity of it is unimaginable. They forage like dogs for food. They eat cockroaches, lice and even rats. They are condemned to lie in their own filth. I beseech you sir to see for yourself. '

Watching the prisoners was a popular pastime. Turnkeys would supplement their salaries by charging visitors an entry fee. Surprisingly, this had official approval. The deterrent effect was supposed to be similar to that of the public hanging.

A Sting In The Tale

One tragic tale sums up the pity of it

.In the 17th. century a young Irish girl, Briony, sold flowers in the city. One of the town's worthies would regularly buy a bunch from her to take home to his wife and daughters.

One day a bee flew out from amongst the flowers and he was stung on the nose. Briony saw the funny side of it, but he didn't. An hour later the girl was arrested on a charge of assault.

The women's cells were full and the unfortunate Briony was forced to share with a dozen men. They were all hardened criminals who were certain to be sentenced to the gallows or transportation.

For more than a week they took it in turns to rape her.

When she was brought to court she was in such a bad state that even with support she was unable to stand and speak for herself. She collapsed and was carried out of the court. Despite the medical attention she now received, Briony died a few hours later.

The Cathedral of St. Nicholas

A Classic Building

Pass Amen Corner on the way to the Cathedral of St. Nicholas.

There has been a church on this site since Norman times. Sections of the present building date back to the 11th. century.

The cathedral was destroyed by fire in 1216 and again in 1248. A new Early English church was complete by 1350 except for the tower with its famous spire and the choir arcades. There was substantial rebuilding during the 19th. century.

The church contains a monument to Lord Collingwood, who was baptized and married here. Collingwood took charge of the fleet at Trafalgar after Nelson was killed. The two naval heroes are buried side by side in St. Paul's

Cathedral. There is also a memorial to a another seafarer, Robert, better known as 'Bobby' Shaftoe, a name once familiar in every nursery and playground in the country.

When the city was attacked by Scots loyal to Cromwell, they threatened to blast the building with cannon. The city's mayor, John Marlay, ordered more than a 100 Scots prisoners to be locked in the building. The message was relayed to the attackers who then concentrated their fire elsewhere.

Many of the Scots prisoners were wounded, and some certainly died during their confinement in the church. The strange sighs and moans often heard around the building have often been said to be associated with this incident.

Hell's Kitchen

Cross to the road opposite the front of the cathedral. This is the Groat Market. Where Thompson House now stands was once the site of Newcastle's most notorious hostelry - the Flying Horse, known as Hell's Kitchen.

At the centre of this crowd of villains was 'Blind Willie' Purvis, a talented fiddler.

Another character was John 'Cuckoo Jack' Wilson whose main occupation was fishing corpses out of the Tyne. Each dead body was worth a handsome dividend. On one occasion he was temporarily overcome with a mood of decency that took him to the aid of a drowning man, but he returned to his senses soon enough and allowed nature to take its course before pulling the body out of the water.

The Groat Market gives onto the Bigg Market. A famous murder took place here outside what is now a Bengal Indian restaurant.

After the second Jacobite rebellion the government agreed that highland soldiers would not have to serve south of the border. However, the agreement was not honoured. One soldier who suffered as a result was young Ewan MacDonald.

Murder At The Bigg Market

On a spring day in 1752 MacDonald, who was serving with the 43rd. Royal Highlanders in Newcastle, entered a Bigg Market hostelry. He was in uniform and he may have anticipated the customary ribald comments.

The young man put up with this. But the insults mounted into a torrent of abuse and finally he could take no more.

As the foul mouthed group walked towards the pub door, MacDonald swung a fist at one of them. His blow connected with a barrel maker called Parker.

The fight spilled into the street. MacDonald took out a gully knife and stabbed Parker in the belly. The young soldier was now fired up into a frenzy. He lashed out at everything in sight, and when the street cleared around him he ran back to the pub and went on the rampage.

He smashed bottles glasses and chairs. His flying feet and fists caused untold bruises and one broken arm. But by the time the militia came to arrest him he was calm, sitting alone in a corner finishing the drink he had paid for when he first crossed the threshold of the inn.

Meanwhile Parker had died on the street. As MacDonald was led away he slid and fell in the pool of blood.

Following the coroner's verdict he was committed for trial. The judge instructed the jury to ignore the provocation. MacDonald was convicted of murder. At the steps of the scaffold MacDonald made a final repentance of his crime. But as he climbed towards the noose, his composure vanished and he tried to throw the hangman off the ladder.

When the rope bit into his neck he kicked wildly again. For more than ten minutes he twitched and twisted and turned. Then suddenly it was all over. The body hung as loose as old sacking.

After a further 10 minutes the body was taken down and placed in a cart. The last stop for local murderers was always the dissection slab at Surgeons' Hall.

The young surgeon who had been lucky enough to be chosen to perform the dissection had been briefly called away to the nearby infirmary. When he returned with a colleague, MacDonald was sitting up on the slab. He looked dazed but was generally not much the worse for his ordeal.

MacDonald begged for mercy. The young surgeon weighed his plea against the lost chance of a dissection. According to the law MacDonald was dead meat, so there was little to consider. The surgeon picked up a heavy mallet and brought it crashing down on the young soldier's skull.

His fellow surgeons agreed that their young colleague had behaved most properly. Indeed, he had shown a great deal of common sense in what was, after all, a tricky situation. To emphasise that these were just the qualities required for one who was to make his living with the saw and scalpel, they decided to make a united gesture.

A special display case was ordered so that all those who entered Surgeons' Hall could have a really good view of the mallet.

Setting A Bad Example

A century earlier there had been another famous killing at the Bigg Market.

Desertions from the king's army had reached epidemic proportions in 1640. When two runaways were arrested and brought to Lord Conway he was determined to use the moment to set an example.

The two men were forced to draw lots. The winner joined the firing squad and the loser was placed against a wall and shot.

As a backbone stiffener this was not successful. At the Battle of Newcastle, Lord Conway's men distinguished themselves only by the speed with which they scattered to escape the enemy.

Walk up the street before crossing over to Newgate Street. Turn left at the camera shop into Clayton Street, then right into Westgate Road.

Although there were occasional hangings at the Sandgate, the more popular sites were the West Gate and Town Moor. The most famous Westgate hangings date from the era of the reivers.** The most elaborate preparations for any Newcastle hanging took place in 1532 when 30 Armstrongs were strung up together.

Leave Westgate Road before the Tyne Theatre and turn up to the right. A right turn from Bath Lane takes you into Stowell Street. The city walls are on the right.

Chinatown

Stowell Street is the heart of Newcastle's Chinatown. It is a delightful place to visit, particularly when lit up for the evening.

Apart from an excellent selection of restaurants there is also an ethnic supermarket. Even the phone boxes have been transformed to give a little extra flavour of the East.

The Black Friars

Turn right opposite the Shangri-La through Jacobins Chare archway. Here are the remains of the Blackfriars monastery. This area is most effectively floodlit each evening.

The monastery was established in the 13th. century but was dissolved on the order of Henry VIII's chief minister, Thomas Cromwell. The friars were ordered to leave the city.

From time to time groups of them would return to the ruins of their monastery. On one occasion three of them were cornered by soldiers loyal to the king. One of them was felled by an axe, and the second run through by a sword. The third managed to run some distance but was finally brought down by an arrow.

It is not surprising that these grounds are regarded as haunted.

The Soccer Capital Of The North

Turn right at Rosie's Bar at the end of Stowell Street. From St. Andrew's Street turn right into Gallowgate.

Part of the region's soccer citadel - Newcastle United's St. James's Park - is the famous Gallowgate Stand. As its name implies, this was also a local hanging site. It is rumoured that the bodies of witches are buried deep beneath the stand.

A Surprising Fact

Saint Andrew's Church is on the right. Access to the churchyard is round the corner. The bodies of the 15 witches hung on the Town Moor in 1650 are buried here.

The churchyard is also the focus of an unusual ghost story.

The Phantom Of The Blue Muslin Dress

A curate based at the church fell for the attractive daughter of a local landowner. It was a relationship fraught with difficulties, the worst of which was that the young man was almost as poor as the proverbial church mouse.

The day after a heated row, the curate was surprised to see the girl walking in the churchyard. He rushed after her, but when he reached the place where she had been standing she'd disappeared.

He went to her home only to find the family in mourning. The girl had fallen downstairs and broken her neck. As far as it was possible to tell this had happened at exactly the moment he had seen her in the churchyard.

The Blackett Street Killing

Cross onto Blackett Street under Eldon Square shopping precinct.

20 years after the Body in the Bank murder, Newcastle was shocked by a similarly strange crime.

Mark Frater was a successful local businessman and tax collector. On the first of October 1861 he travelled to work as usual, arriving at his Blackett Street office at nine o'clock.

He was attacked from behind and stabbed in the throat. The attacker obviously intended to be thorough. He twisted his wrist on the handle several times before withdrawing the bent blade.

Mark Frater staggered into his office clutching his throat. The main artery had been severed, so he hardly had time to announce 'I'm done for' before he was.

A doctor confirmed the death ten minutes later. Meanwhile the attacker, George Clark, had been arrested. He freely admitted his guilt to police and magistrates and took a great interest in newspaper accounts of the killing.

It emerged that he had a deranged grudge against Mark Frater. The taxman had tried to collect a dog licence fee that Clark refused to pay. At the end of the long process of law, Clark had been briefly imprisoned for his continued refusal to pay. He promised himself that when he came out of prison he would kill Mark Frater.

George Clark was sentenced to hang, but won an appeal on the grounds of diminished responsibility. He was sent to an asylum where he remained for the rest of his life.

* See Ghost Trails of Northumbria

** See More Ghost Trails of Northumbria

Historical Notes

A number of important sites and personages are referred to only in passing in the main body of the text. These notes are intended to remedy that omission for those seeking greater clarification of historical contexts.

The information is arranged alphabetically.

ARMSTRONG, WILLIAM GEORGE, 1ST BARON (1810-1900) Archetypal Victorian entrepreneur on a grand scale. Also scientist, inventor, engineer and student of natural history. Managed to sell his Armstrong gun to both sides in the American Civil War, yet also had the vision to transform his country home, Cragside, near Rothbury, by a series of plantings that would not come to full fruition until after his death.

BALLIOL, JOHN, KING OF SCOTLAND. (1292-6, b.1250) Great-great nephew of William the Lion (qv), his status as a subject of Edward I (qv) made his position untenable. He rebelled against Edward, but was defeated by him at the Battle of Dunbar in 1295.

BANNOCKBURN, BATTLE OF. In June 1314 Edward II (qv) led an army of 20,000 men to relieve Stirling Castle. Robert the Bruce (qv) intercepted them with a much smaller force and the English came second.

BOLEYN, ANNE (1507 - 1536) Married Henry VIII (qv) in 1533 when already pregnant by him. Had the misfortune to bear a daughter and then fail to produce a son, so was beheaded on trumped up charges to make way for the already-pregnant Jane Seymour.

CARHAM, BATTLE OF, (1018). Malcolm II of Scotland (qv) heavily defeated Edred of Northumbria on the Tweed, thus permanently securing Lothian for Scotland.

CHARLEMAGNE, KING OF THE FRANKS, (771 - 814 b. 742) Conquered most of Western Europe in a campaign that lasted almost 30 years. Managed to keep in with the popes of the time and so was crowned Holy Roman Emperor.

CIVIL WAR, THE ENGLISH (1642 - 1651) More properly called the Civil Wars. The culmination of the deterioration in the relationship between the crown and the parliament through the reigns of James I and Charles I, and the financial and religious policies of Charles in particular, triggered rebellion in Scotland and Ireland. The short and long parliaments of 1640 demanded reform which included parliamentary control over the king's choice of advisors.

In January 1642 Charles failed to secure the arrest of five members of parliament and quit the capital. He set up his standard at Nottingham in August of the same year. The royalists enjoyed early success in battles at Edgehill, Newcastle and Hopton, but failed to consolidate these victories. Scottish troops under Argyll entered England and contributed to the first parliamentary success at Marston Moor. Argyll's troops were withdrawn to deal with a royalist uprising in Scotland and an indecisive battle was fought at Newbury.

In 1645 Fairfax's New Model Army inflicted a major defeat on the royalists at Naseby. In 1648 revolts in the south anticipated further intervention by the Scots on the king's behalf. Fairfax crushed the rebellion in the south and Cromwell (qv) defeated the invading Scots at Preston. Charles was tried by a court set up by the Rump Parliament and executed on 30th. January 1649. In 1650 Cromwell inflicted a final defeat on the Scots at Dunbar, and in the following year Charles II's invading army was crushed at Worcester. The Commonwealth formed to govern the country at the end of the war lasted until Booth's Rising and the Restoration of 1660.

COLLINGWOOD, CUTHBERT, Ist BARON (1759 - 1810). Born in Newcastle upon Tyne, he joined the navy at the age of 11 and rose to the rank of Admiral. He fought outstandingly during the Napoleonic Wars and took over from Nelson after the latter's death at Trafalgar.

CROMWELL, OLIVER (1599 - 1658). Represented Huntingdon in the parliament of 1628 and Cambridge in the Short and Long Parliaments. He was 43 at the outbreak of the Civil War and in three years rose from the rank of captain to lieutenant-general. He created and moulded a superb cavalry force and replaced Fairfax as lord-general in 1650. He defended the Commonwealth at Dunbar and Worcester and became Lord Protector and Head of State in 1653. Despite his reforming zeal and expert military leadership, Oliver Cromwell is best remembered as the prime mover in the trial and execution of King Charles I.

CROMWELL, THOMAS, EARL OF ESSEX. (1485 - 1540) A clever schemer, he continued to find favour with Henry VIII (qv) after the downfall of his master, Cardinal Wolsey. He drafted the legislation that seceded the Church of England from Rome, thereby gaining Henry a divorce from Katherine of Aragon. Later he masterminded the dissolution of the monasteries which led to the Pilgrimage of Grace (qv). His downfall came because he was the chief negotiator who secured Anne of Cleves as a wife for Henry. Another Tudor victim of trumped up charges, he was executed for treason.

DAVID I, KING OF SCOTLAND. (1124 -53, b. 1084) Anglo-Norman son of Malcolm Conmore who was responsible for the spread of the Feudal System in Scotland and the rise of other great Anglo-Norman families such as the Balliols and Bruces. He was a fervent supporter of the church, encouraged its reorganisation along diocesan and parochial lines and founded many great abbeys. A supporter of his niece Matilda against Stephen (qv) he managed to secure Northumberland from Stephen despite losing the Battle of the Standard

DERWENTWATER, JAMES RADCLIFFE, 3rd EARL OF (1689 - 1716). Brought up in the French court as companion to James Stuart, the Old Pretender, he returned to England in 1710 to live on his English estates. He joined in the rebellion of 1715, but escaped arrest through the devotion of his tenants. In October 1715, he joined Tom Forster at Greenrigg and together they went to Preston where the Jacobites lost a battle and the Earl was captured. He was beheaded on Tower Hill in February 1716.

EDWARD I, KING OF ENGLAND (1272 - 1307 b. 1229). Considering he listed his chief interests as legislation and crusading, he did a fantastic job of annexing Wales and conquering Scotland. His downfall, like many a statesman's after him, was his over-zealous raising of taxes to pay for his reforms and wars. The 'Hammer of the Scots' died near Carlisle whilst preparing yet another invasion.

EDWARD II (1307 - 1327, b 1284). Edward's reign was punctuated by famine, failures in war and baronial opposition. His extravagance and homosexuality made him unpopular, but the murder of a favourite (Gaveston) in 1312 destroyed the united face of the opposition. He suffered humiliating defeats at Bannockburn (qv) and in France and new opposition grew around his queen, Isabella, and Roger Mortimer. Edward was deposed and brutally murdered in September 1327.

EDWARD III, KING OF ENGLAND (1327-1377 b.1312) Began his reign by imprisoning his mother and executing her lover, Roger Mortimer. Militarily unsuccessful in Scotland, he turned his attention to France, started the Hundred Years War, and promptly lost, despite the brilliancy at Crecy, Calais and Poitiers. Since he was so occupied with military matters, his reign saw a significant increase in the role of Parliament.

EDWARD IV (1461 - 1470, 1471 - 83, b 1442). A brave and popular soldier during the Wars of the Roses. He won a significant victory at Towton (1461), but his marriage to Elizabeth Woodville alienated his mentor, Warwick the Kingmaker. He was driven into exile but returned to lead a successful campaign in March 1471. He gave England domestic peace but failed to reconcile disputes at court. The most important of these, between the Woodvilles and the Duke of Gloucester [the future Richard III (qv)] caused further strife after his death.

EDWARD VI, KING OF ENGLAND (1547 - 1553 b. 1537). Son of Henry VIII and Jane Seymour, Edward was an ardent Protestant and was much influenced by the Dukes of Somerset and Northumberland. It is possible that he initiated the plot to proclaim Lady Jane Grey Queen in place of his half-sister

Mary, who was a Catholic. His other half sister, Elizabeth, (qv) was a Protestant, too.

ELIZABETH I, QUEEN OF ENGLAND (1558 - 1603, b 1533). In 1536 her mother, Anne Boleyn, (qv) was executed in the Tower on the order of her father, Henry VIII (qv). Elizabeth herself was imprisoned in the Tower during the reign of her half-sister, Mary. Her political astuteness helped her not only to survive, but to become one of England's most celebrated monarchs. Her reign brought peace, and a measure of religious settlement until the War with Spain in 1585.

The scuttling of the Armada settled that conflict, but revolts in Ireland and the Earl of Essex's rebellion were symptoms of unresolved difficulties. These seeds of discontent culminated in Civil War (qv) of 1642 and the end of absolute monarchy in Britain.

GREY, CHARLES, 2nd EARL (1764 - 1845). British Prime Minister from 1830 to 1834, it was under his administration that the first Reform Bill was passed. It is his monument that overlooks Grey Street & Grey's Square in Newcastle and after whom the tea is named. He fell out of favour with the Hanoverian kings after declaring that the monarchy should demonstrate its fitness to govern.

HALIDON HILL, BATTLE OF (19th July 1333) Fought during the siege of Berwick by Edward III (qv) and Edward Balliol against Sir Archibald Douglas. The result of the battle was decisive, though it served no real purpose in the long-running saga of Scottish Independence.

HEDGELEY MOOR, BATTLE OF (1464). A stone marks the spot where Sir Ralph Percy fell. Hedgeley Moor was a decisive Yorkist victory during the Wars of the Roses. The Percys changed their allegiance several times, unfortunately ending up on the losing side.

HENRY VI (1422 - 1461, 1470 - 71, b 1421). Succeeded to the thrones of England and France before his first birthday. He came of age in 1456 but showed little inclination for ruling. He was dominated by the Duke of Suffolk and his wife, Margaret of Anjou. His decline into insanity precipitated the Wars of the Roses. On his restoration he became a pawn of Warwick the Kingmaker. After Warwick's fall Henry was captured at Barnet, confined to the Tower, and murdered on the orders of King Edward IV (qv).

HENRY VIII (1509 - 47, b 1491). Henry came to the throne with little political or governmental experience. He learned these skills quickly and presided over one of the most lavish and cultured courts in Europe. His decision to divorce Katherine of Aragon created a division with Rome and the establishment of the Church of England. He was always the final power in government but had little taste for administration. This was left to famous servants, notably the three Thomas' - More, Cromwell (qv), and Wolsey - all of whom suffered considerably after falling from the king's favour. Henry is now best remembered for his six wives and as the composer of Greensleeves.

HOTSPUR, SIR HENRY PERCY. (1364 - 1403) Son of the Earl of Northumberland, Hotspur was particularly zealous in guarding the borders. Captured by the Scots at Otterburn (1388), he later helped Henry IV to the throne, won a victory for him at Homildon Hill (1402), but changed sides and died at the Battle of Shrewsbury (1403). Hotspur, who has near legendary status in Northumberland, was portrayed as a contemporary of Prince Henry (later Henry V) by Shakespeare. He was in fact 23 years older than the prince. But the near sibling rivalry between the two 'young men' is an important theme in Henry IV Part One. Shakespeare climaxes the play with Prince Hal locked in mortal combat with Hotspur on the battlefield. The fatal blow provokes the words - ' Oh Harry! Thou hast robbed me of my youth.' Hotspur was killed a few months before his 40th. birthday.

JACOBITES is the name given to the supporters of the deposed James II (VII of Scotland) and his son, James. Jacobite plots began in 1688, but the first serious threat to the Hanoverian succession came in 1715. This was the Earl of Mar's Scottish rising, which was supported by Northumberland's Thomas Forster and the Earl of Derwentwater (qv). The rebels reached Preston where they capitulated.

The more serious affair was in 1745. 'Bonnie Prince Charlie' had landed in Scotland two years previously with 10,000 French troops. The standard was raised at Glenfinnan in '45 and support came mainly from the west and central highlands. The prince captured Perth and Edinburgh, and a victory at Prestonpans encouraged him to march into the heart of England. The expected support did not materialise and the prince turned back at Derby. There was a last victory at Falkirk before the slaughter of the highlanders at Culloden Moor. Prince Charles escaped with his life, but the Jacobite cause was lost.

JAMES VI & I, KING OF SCOTLAND (1567 - 1625) KING OF GREAT BRITAIN (1603 - 1625) b. 1566. Became King at a very tender age when his mother, Mary, Queen of Scots (qv) was forced to abdicate. His father, Darnley having been murdered with his mother's connivance, James was left in the care of a variety of Scottish nobles. A shrewd and flexible diplomat, James managed to tame the wilder excesses of his nobles and keep the church in check also. Hailed as a great King of Scotland, his reputation as a king in England after his accession to the throne was decidedly dodgy. He was seen as a drunken, foul mouthed, undignified coward with homosexual leanings. His financial irresponsibility, pro Spanish foreign policy and continuous assertions of royal authority led to a deterioration of relations between Parliament and the monarchy which led ultimately to the execution of his son, Charles I.

JEFFRIES, JUDGE. Following Monmouth's 1685 rebellion against James II, Chief Justice Jeffries presided over a large number of assize courts (known as the Bloody Assizes) where over 1,000 rebels were brutally treated. This did not endear him, or the king, to the general populace.

JOHN, KING OF ENGLAND (1199 - 1216, b. 1167). Younger brother of Richard the Lionheart (qv), he was Regent in his brother's absence. Not content with succeeding to the throne of England, he renewed the war with France and lost most of the English possessions there. His objections to the Pope's nomination for Archbishop of Canterbury led to his excommunication in 1212. His objections to the power of his barons led to Magna Carta in 1215. Not so much the monster portrayed by history as a weak and stubborn man, with a cruel streak.

MALCOLM II, KING OF SCOTLAND (1005 - 1034) Victor at the Battle of Carham (qv), he also gained control over Strathclyde and thus effectively completed the unification of Scotland. Today he is more likely to be remembered as the grandfather of Macbeth, who murdered his cousin and Malcolm's successor, Duncan.

MARY, QUEEN OF SCOTS (1542 - 1587). Three times married mother of James VI & I, she is often implicated in the plot which led to the murder of her second husband, Darnley, through the agency of her third, James Hepburn, Earl of Bothwell. She was a constant thorn in the side of her cousin, Elizabeth I (qv) who eventually gained sufficient evidence to convince her that Mary was attempting to become Queen and had her executed.

OTTERBURN, BATTLE OF (5th August 1388). Scots raiding party under James, Earl of Douglas were attacked by Hotspur (qv) at dusk. Douglas was killed, Hotspur taken prisoner and victory claimed by the Scots. Also known as 'The Battle by Moonlight' and 'Chevy Chase'.

PILGRIMAGE OF GRACE (1536). An essentially peaceful uprising - or rather series of uprisings - in the North of England against the dissolution of the monasteries and in support of the Catholic church. Led by Robert Aske, 35,000 men marched on Doncaster where they were met by Henry VIII's (qv) emissary, the Duke of Norfolk. Talks were held and the men dispersed. Further minor uprisings in 1537 led to severe repression and the execution of Robert Aske.

RICHARD I, KING OF ENGLAND, 'THE LIONHEART' (1189 - 1199, b. 1157) A son of Henry II, he spent only 6 months of his reign in England, preferring his French castles when he wasn't away at the Crusades. His brother, John, (qv) was Regent in his absence and tried to take the throne for himself.

RICHARD III (1483 - 1485, b. 1452). Gained fame, but never popularity, as a soldier whilst his brother, Edward IV (qv) was king. Shakespeare has him portrayed as a hunchbacked monster, responsible for the murder of the Princes in the Tower. There is no evidence that he was hunchbacked, but it was certainly politically expedient for Henry VII to have him maligned and hence he became the victim of more Tudor trumped-up charges.

ROBERT THE BRUCE, KING OF SCOTLAND (1306 - 1329, b. 1274). After swearing allegiance to Edward I (qv), changed his mind and made a bid for an independent Scottish kingdom. Conducted a guerilla war and used scorched-earth tactics until finally he inflicted a crushing defeat on Edward II (qv) at Bannockburn (qv). He only got his heart's desire after the death of Edward II, when both the English and the Pope finally accepted Scottish independence.

STEPHEN, KING OF ENGLAND (1135 - 1154, b. 1100). Grandson of William the Conqueror (qv) who fought a desultory civil war for the crown of England against his cousin Matilda (daughter of the previous king, Henry I and granddaughter of William the Conqueror). Upon the death of his only son in 1153, Stephen was forced to name Matilda's son, the future Henry II as his successor.

WILLIAM I, KING OF ENGLAND, 'THE CONQUEROR' (1066 - 87, b. 1028). Illegitimate son of a Duke of Normandy, he succeeded his father in 1035 and then pursued a series of campaigns, the most famous of which is the one that led him to become King of England after the Battle of Hastings. The Anglo-Norman state he created during a time of almost permanent rebellion and as recorded in Domesday Book - essentially a statement of tax liability - survived as his chief memorial.

WILLIAM II, KING OF ENGLAND, 'THE RUFUS' (1087 - 1100, b. 1057). The third, but favourite son of William the Conqueror (qv), he was handed the throne despite the claims of his elder brother Robert, who had rebelled against their father. He is remembered as a cruel tyrant who was mysteriously killed whilst hunting in the New Forest, possibly at the instigation of his younger brother, the future Henry I

WILLIAM THE LION, KING OF SCOTLAND (1165 - 1214. Born 1143). A younger brother of Malcolm IV, he joined the alliance against Henry II, but his invasion led only to his capture at Alnwick in 1174. He bought a pardon from Richard I (qv), then failed ignominiously to wrest the borders from John (qv).

Pauperhaugh Bridge